The Veggie Grower's Bible

Lorraine Burn

First published 2010
Activity Plus Limited, Derbyshire. DE56 4WZ
01332 842313

ISBN: 978 0954 9072 8 0

CONTENTS

The aim of this book is to make things quick and easy to understand.

The easy/tricky options give an indicator of the expected skill level required to grow the particular vegetable: easy or tricky!

Generally, once you have prepared the soil (see the crop rotation and bed preparation sections) most of the difficulty is in the amount of time and attention a particular crop will need – this is defined by the star ratings.

Star Rating

*	This is the easiest type of all! Almost, just put in the ground and leave until harvesting.
**	A small amount of attention needed, watch for bugs and water if dry.
***	Some amount of regular attention needed.
****	Regular care and attention needed.
*****	Lots of attention needed.

KEY TO SYMBOLS AND TERMS

	Water until plants are well established
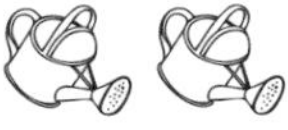	Water generously in dry spells
	Keep well watered
	Protect from frost
	Site in full sun
	Site in partial shade
	Add compost in Spring (See P.8/9 for soil guides)
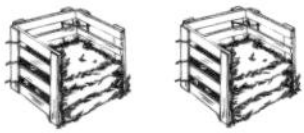	Add lots of compost in Spring (See P.8/9 for soil guides)
	Manure in Spring A large wheel barrow approx. 50kg (110lbs) covers 7-8m^2

 (1-2)	Add a general fertilizer of your choice 1 week (dependent on number displayed) before planting
	Stake securely
W	Keep weed free
	Cover with a cloche
	Protect from slugs and snails
L	Lime if soil is acidic
 /	Sow under glass/unheated greenhouse
	Plant out glass grown seedling/plant
	Heated greenhouse
	Protect from birds/net
	Protect from butterflies/caterpillars

SOIL

It is well worthwhile paying particular attention to your soil. Best results come from understanding what individual crops need or don't need – soil preparation really is the secret to success.

Ideally, your soil should:

- ✔ Be fine enough to plant seeds (may need rotovating).
- ✔ Contain sufficient nutrients to feed the vegetables.
- ✔ Be limed well enough to keep down acidity levels.
- ✔ Be free draining enough to prevent water logging.

Type	Quick description	To improve add
Sand	Very free draining and fast to warm up in the spring.	
Loam	Free draining, fast to warm up in the spring. Lovely soil!	
Silt	A little sticky, but retains water and nutrients well.	
Clay	Waterlogs in winter, cracks in summer. Cold soil and heavy to dig!	L Add drainage
Peat	Can be slow to drain and often too acidic for vegetables alone	L
Chalky	Free draining and often too alkaline for vegetables alone.	

Compost, well rotted manure and fertilizers are essential for improving the structure and fertility of all soils. Leaf mould and old mushroom compost are also very useful.

Topsoil: The darkest layer of soil which holds all the organic matter that feeds the plants. The ideal depth of top soil for growing vegetables is 45-60cm (18"-2ft).

Sub soil: Usually lighter in colour, containing no plant nutrients. Loosen/dig in autumn to keep soil healthy and productive. Don't mix with topsoil!

A soil testing kit will quickly tell you what type of soil you have and its pH value.

pH VALUES	
1.0	Extremely acidic
4.0	Maximum acidity tolerated by most plants
5.5	Maximum acidity tolerated by most vegetables
6.5	Grows the best vegetables
7.0	Neutral, maximum alkalinity for vegetables
14.0	Extremely alkaline

Once you have the soil as you want it, the easiest method for ensuring that particular plants have their nutritional needs met is to practice crop rotation. (See crop rotation section).

FERTILISING

Fertilising is an absolute minefield! Too much is not good, too little is worse! You need to understand your NPK's.

Assuming you have prepared your ground as required (by adding manure etc. see crop rotation charts), quick growing crops should be fine on one application of general fertilizer. Plants that take longer to grow will benefit from another application half way through their growing cycle.

N	Nitrogen	Plant growth, leaves etc
P	Phosphorous	Root growth and ripening of fruit
K	Potassium (Potash)	Flowering and formation of fruit

Natural fertilisers: tend to break down slowly so provide their nutrients over a longer period.

Artificial fertilisers: are a more specific way to correct soil conditions and should only be used when you know exactly what is required. Always read packet instructions for application.

Compound artificial fertilisers: combine artificial fertilisers in varying amounts and are generally used for particular crop needs.

Liquid fertilisers: are a good, quick feed as nutrients are delivered into the soil for immediate use by the plants.

% NPK Values	N	P	K
Natural Animal Fertilisers			
Horse Manure (likely values)	0.6	0.3	0.6
Chicken Manure (likely values)	1.5	1	0.5
Rabbit Manure (likely values)	2.5	1.4	0.6
Natural Fertilisers			
Bloodmeal and Hoof and Horn	12		
Bonemeal	3.5	18	0
Chicken Manure Pellets	4	2.5	2
Fish, Blood and Bone	6	6	6
Compound Artificial Fertilisers			
Growmore	7	7	7
Hydro Complex	12	11	18
Vitax Q4	5.3	7.5	10
Artificial Fertilisers			
Sulphate of Ammonia	20		
Prilled Urea	46		
Nitrate of Soda	16		
Sulphate of Potash			50
Rock Phosphate		26	
Superphosphate		18.5	

Home made compost (likely values)	0.5	0.25	0.8

Well rotted manure is animal manure that has been left in a heap for at least 1 year. It should be dark, crumbly, look and feel like compost. *Never use fresh manure* - it will ‘burn’ plant roots. Never mix with lime immediately and always leave a few months between applications. Lime in the autumn and manure in the early spring.

Crop Rotation

Rotating your crops is just good sense. It is an environmentally friendly way to help prevent soil pests that thrive with a particular crop. It also allows different crop families to use the particular nutrients in the soil that they specifically need.

Main family groups: (these colour codes refer to the 3 year plan).

Allium	Onion, leek, shallot, garlic types
Brassica	Cauliflower, broccoli, kale, swede, radish types
Cucurbit	Cucumber, marrow, pumpkin, courgette types
Legume	Bean, pea types
Potato	Potato, tomato, aubergine types
Umbelliferae (Roots)	Carrot, parsnip, parsley, celery types

Lettuce, salad leaves, salsify and sweet corn can be planted with any family. The main principle is – do not grow the same plants in the same place for at least 2 years.

Brassicas follow 'Others', beans in particular, because of their nitrogen fixing qualities.

The easiest and probably most commonly used is the 3 Year Plan. After taking out the permanent beds the available space is then divided up into 3 sections.

Year 1
Roots
Others
Brassicas
Permanent

Year 2
Brassicas
Roots
Others
Permanent

Year 3
Others
Brassicas
Roots
Permanent

What to apply to each bed each year	
Roots:	1-2 if needed
Others:	1-2
Brassicas:	L 1-2
Permanent:	Generally top dress

A crop rotation plan to aspire to...

This plan works well if you have the space.

Year 1	Year 2	Year 3
Potatoes	Roots	Alliums
Legumes	Potatoes	Roots
Brassicas	Legumes	Potatoes
Cucurbit	Brassicas	Legumes
Alliums	Cucurbits	Brassicas
Roots	Alliums	Cucurbits
Permanent	Permanent	Permanent

After Year 6, return to the first group.

Year 4	Year 5	Year 6
Cucurbits	Brassicas	Legumes
Alliums	Cucurbits	Brassicas
Roots	Alliums	Cucurbits
Potatoes	Roots	Alliums
Legumes	Potatoes	Roots
Brassicas	Legumes	Potatoes
Permanent	Permanent	Permanent

Make a plan

It really is the easiest way to make sure you keep on top of your crop rotation. Start with what you want to grow this year. I want to grow…

Fruit	Raspberries, Gooseberries, Rhubarb (Permanent)
Roots	Carrots, Parsnips, Beetroots, Salsify, Hamburg Parsley, Chinese Artichokes
Legumes	Beans – Broad, Runner, Purple Climbing, Green Climbing, Peas, Chard, Spinach
Potatoes	First Earlies
Brassicas	Kale – Dwarf, Red, Calabrese, Sprouts, Green Cauliflower, Kohl Rabi, Swedes
Alliums	Garlic, Onions, Leeks, Spring Onions
Cucurbits	Courgettes, Patty Pans, Pointed Squash, Butternut, Mini sweet corn
Herbs	Parsley, Chives, Mint, Lemon Balm
Salads	Lettuce, Pak Choi
Flowers	Sweet Peas, Dahlias, Gladioli, Carnations

Then all you have to do is roughly sketch your available space, divide it into the appropriate areas and fill in the details. The most difficult thing is keeping to it!

Tips: Keep a little space for things you have forgotten, get given or discover after you have prepared your plan.

*Keep your old plans to refer to for the following years.

Sample Plan

Bed 1

Raspberries	Broad Beans/Winter Cabbage (following on)	
	Runner Beans	Climbing Purple Beans

Bed 2

Salads	Peas Spinach	Chard	**Spare to be filled**

Bed 3

Parsnips	Hamburg Parsley	Scorzonera Salsify

Bed 4

Sprouting Broccoli	Green Cauliflower	Red Kale
	POTATOES-FIRST EARLIES	
	Calabrese	Curly Kale

Bed 5

Mini Corn		Patty Pan	Mini Corn	
Mini Corn	Courgette	Mini Corn	Mini Corn	Squash
Courgette	Mini Corn		Butternut	Mini Corn

Bed 6

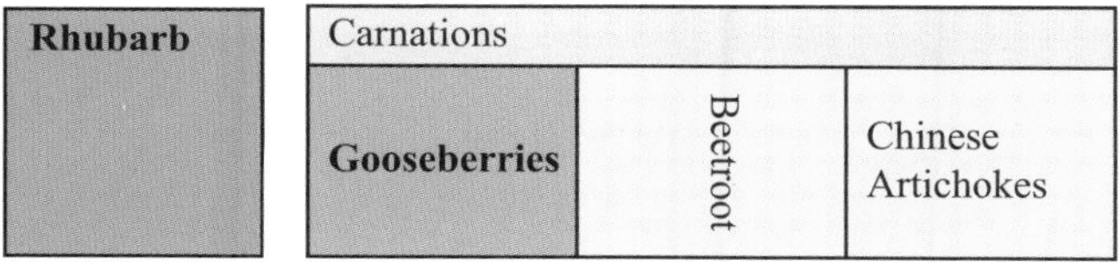

Rhubarb

Carnations

Gooseberries

Beetroot

Chinese Artichokes

Bed 7

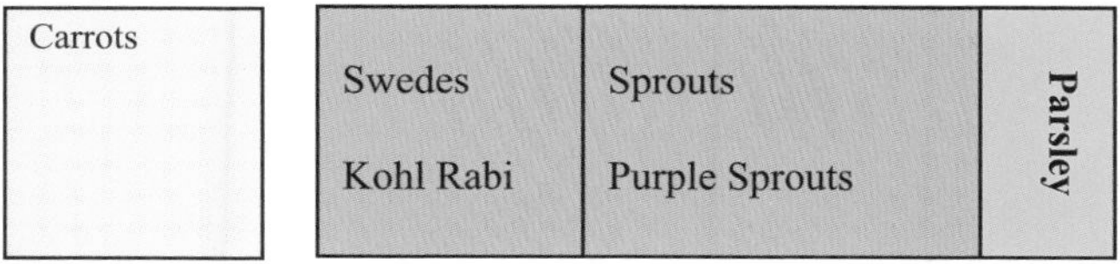

Carrots

Swedes

Kohl Rabi

Sprouts

Purple Sprouts

Parsley

Bed 8

ONIONS

Chives

Bed 9

Spring Onions

LEEKS

Mint

Bed 10

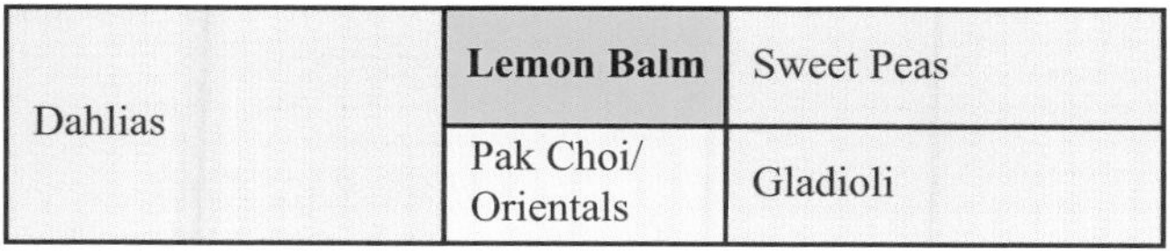

Dahlias

Lemon Balm

Sweet Peas

Pak Choi/ Orientals

Gladioli

Prepare an Allium bed

Seedbed: You will only need to prepare a seedbed to raise leeks and onions from seed rather than sets. These seeds need a finely tilthed soil which has plenty of humus and organic matter.
Main bed: The alliums all need humus rich, well-drained soil. Dig over in autumn. In spring mix in a reasonable amount of organic matter or compost and rake the surface to make level. You are aiming for a reasonably fine surface or crumb structure. 1-2 weeks before planting, mix a general fertilizer into the soil 5-7cm (2-3") deep.

Alliums which are in the ground for a long time will benefit from a liquid feed occasionally.

Prepare a Root bed

The two main things to remember with a root bed are:
i) It does not need to be too rich: too many nutrients will cause the plant to do more than you want. Splitting, forking or abundant leaf growth will follow, giving disappointing edible results.
ii) It needs to be dug deeply and be free from stones and debris.

Dig over well in autumn. In spring and add organic matter if your soil looks starved of nutrients and rake the surface to make level. As root crops are generally sown in their final growing position, you are aiming for a reasonably fine crumb structure to give your roots a good start. 2 weeks before sowing, apply a light dressing of general purpose fertiliser.

Prepare a Legume bed

Legumes like a free root run and moist, well draining soil rich in organic matter. They will crop heavily if happy.

In autumn, dig over the bed to at least one forks depth and loosen the soil beneath that. In spring add organic matter or compost.

2 weeks before sowing or planting out, mix in a general purpose fertiliser up to 15cm (6") deep.

Prepare a Herb Salad bed

Herbs generally like free draining soil enriched with plenty of organic matter. General bed preparation is to dig over thoroughly in autumn. Work in plenty of organic matter in the spring. Add a top dressing of general fertiliser 1 week before planting out in spring.

Prepare a Cucurbit bed

Cucurbits like a free root run and a moist, free draining soil that is rich in organic matter, they also need full sun.

Dig over the bed well in autumn. In the spring, dig individual 'stations' 30 x 30, and 30cm deep (12 x 12 x 12") and fill with compost/manure. Level the dug out top soil and either form a small circular ridge around the filled hole to help retain water or bury a 15cm (6") approx pot to its rim ready to fill with water when needed. Mix in a general fertiliser 2 week before planting.

Prepare a Brassica bed

Seedbed: Most brassicas are sown in a separate bed before being planted out into their final positions. They take a long time to mature, so using a seedbed allows a more efficient use of space whilst seedlings are growing.

Use any sheltered, sunny location you have and ensure that the seedlings are planted in fertile soil to give them a good start. Lots of extra compost mixed into the soil is good! When transplanting seedlings, use a fork to lift, ensuring minimum root disturbance and leave as much soil on the roots as you can.

Main Bed: Time and effort spent on preparing a bed for your brassicas will be well rewarded. Brassicas are a hungry crop due to the production of lots of big leaves and heads. To support the growth of these plants, the soil needs to be very rich in both nitrogen and humus. Sprouts and cabbage particularly enjoy very high nitrogen levels.

Dig over the soil in autumn, lime if necessary. In spring add lots of manure (compost will also work). Mix into the top 20cm (8") and leave. Brassicas do best in soil with a pH of 6.5-7.5.

1-2 weeks before planting apply a general fertilizer to the prepared bed; carefully rake in because brassicas need to grow in firm soil.

Even after all this preparation, it may be necessary to apply another high nitrogen feed halfway through the growing cycle. Little cardboard 'collars' are useful for placing around the stems of newly transplanted seedlings to protect from pests.

Prepare a Potato bed

Potatoes are reputed to be a crop that will grow anywhere in any soil. It is said that potatoes will break down horrible soil and leave it ready for other crops. Although there may be some element of truth in this theory, you still require soil dug well enough to plant your tubers, be able to earth them up and have enough nutrients to sustain a crop.

It is true, however, that if you dig over your potato bed in the autumn and add plenty of manure/compost before planting in the spring, you will definitely get a higher yielding crop.

Maintaining Permanent beds

Permanent beds need occasional attention too! It is always easier to remove weeds as you see them appear throughout the year, but in autumn, remove any perennial weeds whilst you have the chance and apply a top dressing of well rotted manure, leaf mould or compost.

In spring, keep on top of the weeds and sprinkle a general purpose fertiliser

Companion Planting

Companion planting is an eco-friendly way to prevent pests taking over and should be considered as an important weapon for pest control. However, some companion planting can harm the well being of other plants – study the avoid columns.

Companion planting works on 4 main principles:

1. Scent and camouflage

   Some plants produce scents and chemicals to protect themselves from pests and can therefore be useful/ disastrous for other plants.The scents also simply work on a confusion basis,e.g. mint confuses carrot root fly.

2. Sacrificial

   Some plants specifically attract certain insects; the concept here is to plant one crop to save another e.g. black fly love nasturtiums over broad beans.

3. Allies

   Some plants attract beneficial insects that will devour nuisance pests; e.g. marigolds attract hoverflies which love aphids.

4. Repellent

   Certain strong smells repel insects; e.g. ants hate tansy.

The Three Sisters approach is a traditional Native American companion planting suggestion using corn, squash and beans.... Beans provide nitrogen for the corn, the corn provides support for the squash and beans.

Flower	Attracts	Repels	Plant with
Cosmos	Pollinators, Bees		Almost everything
Dahlia	Nematodes, Earwigs		Almost everything
French Marigolds	Pollinators	Several insects, Soil Nematodes	Almost everything
Limnanthes (Poached Egg Plant)	Hoverflies, Lacewings		Almost everything
Calendula (Pot Marigolds)			Almost everything
Nasturtium		Aphids	Almost everything Cabbage Cucurbits
Nicotiana			Almost everything
Californian Poppy	Pollinators	Aphids	Almost everything
Sunflowers	Ants Herd Aphids, Birds		Almost everything
Sweet Peas	Pollinators	Aphids	Almost everything
Tagetes	Pollinators	Carrot fly	Almost everything

Vegetable combinations to avoid

Vegetable	Avoid - Do not plant with
Beans	Onion, Basil, Kohl Rabi, Fennel, Basil
Cabbage	Tomato, Strawberry, Beans
Carrots	Celery, Parsnip, Dill
Celery	Carrot, Parsley, Parsnip
Cucumbers	Potato
Peas	Potato, Beans, Sage
Potato	Kohl Rabi, Parsnip, Turnip

Herbs - most popular

Herb	Attracts	Repels	Plant with	Avoid
Basil	Butterflies	Flies, Mosquitoes	Tomatoes Peppers	
Borage	Pollinators		Everything	
Chamomile	Hoverflies		Cabbage, Onions	

Herb	Attracts	Repels	Plant with	Avoid
Coriander		Aphids	Spinach	
Chives		Carrot fly, Aphids	Carrots	Beans, Peas
Dill	Pollinators	Aphids, Spider Mite	Cabbage Onions, Lettuce	Carrots, Tomatoes
Garlic		Aphids, Ants		
Lavender	Pollinators	Biting insects		
Lemon Balm	Bees			
Mint	Brassicas	Carrot fly, Flea beetles, Cabbage fly, Ants, Aphids		
Parsley	Insects			
Penny-Royal		Flies, Mosquitoes		
Rosemary	Pollinators	Bean pests Carrot root fly		
Sage	Bees	Slugs, Carrot root fly,	Cabbage, Carrots	Cucumber
Tansy		Flying insects, Ants, Flies		Brassicas
Thyme	Insects			

Artichoke - Globe

A large hungry and thirsty perennial plant that needs lots of space as it can grow up to 1.5m (5ft). Globe artichokes are easiest and fastest grown from rooted suckers as seeds are difficult to germinate, fiddly and very time consuming.

Care:

- ✔ Mulch around the base of plants in late spring.
- ✔ Give a liquid feed every 3-4 weeks.
- ✔ Cut stems down to 45cm (18") in November.
- ✔ Renew plants every 3-4 years.

Pests: Slugs, aphids (on young plants).

Diseases: Petal blight.

Harvesting:

Harvest from 2+ year old plants. Cut heads when large and swollen but still closed, leaving 5-7cm (2-3") of stalk. Start from the top of the plant and work down.

Tip: Young leaf shoots are a little like celery and are also edible.

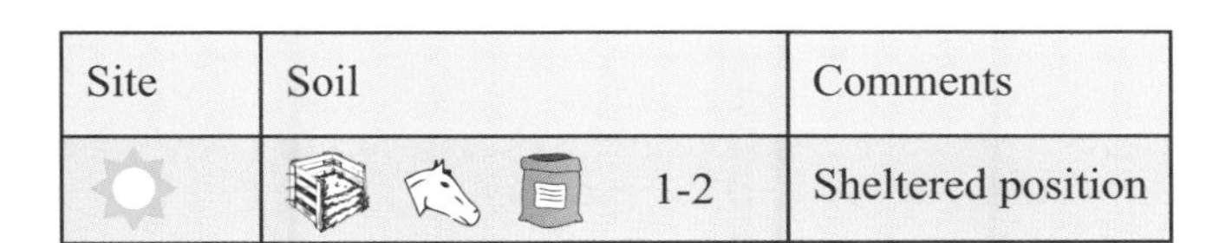

Site	Soil	Comments
	1-2	Sheltered position

Yield (mature plants)	8-10 heads
Planting to plate	72 weeks ($1^1/_2$ years)

Planting:

Use well rooted plants which are at least 25-30cm (9-12") tall.

	J	F	M	A	M	J	J	A	S	O	N	D
Sow				■■	■□							
Eat							■■	■■	■■			

Spacing:

90cm apart x 90cm between rows (3ft x 3ft) at least 5-8cm (2-3") deep.

Side growths or rooted suckers can be taken from existing plants and planted into individual pots of compost in April or November to root. If you plant young suckers each year you can keep a stock of 2-3 year old plants that gives best yields.

Artichoke - Jerusalem

A tall hardy perennial plant with sunflower like, yellow flowers. Tubers are knobbly and uneven and resemble a potato in shape. They have a mild taste that is vaguely similar to globe artichokes and you can expect to harvest tubers up to 10cm (4") and 5cm (2") round. These plants will easily reach 2.5m (10ft).

Care:

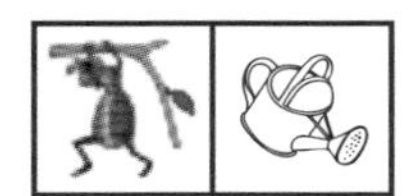

- ✔ Remove flower heads as they appear.
- ✔ Ensure all tubers are dug up whilst harvesting as they will reappear next season.
- ✔ Earth up when plants reach 30-45cm (12-18").

Pests: Slugs, aphids (on young plants).
Diseases: Sclerotina disease.

Harvesting:

Once the leaves have turned brown and died down in October, cut down stems to 30cm (12") and lift as required.

Beware!
A row of Jerusalem Artichokes will form a heavily shaded wall robbing smaller plants of light, space and nutrients.

Site	Soil	Comments
	Almost any	Must not be waterlogged or acidic

Approx germination	14-28 days
Planting to plate	45 weeks

Planting:

Use small tubers approximately the size of a golf ball.

	J		F		M		A		M		J		J		A		S		O		N		D	
Sow				■	■	■	■																	
Eat	■	■	■	■																■	■	■	■	■

Spacing:

45cm apart x 90cm (18 x 3ft) at least 15cm (6") deep.

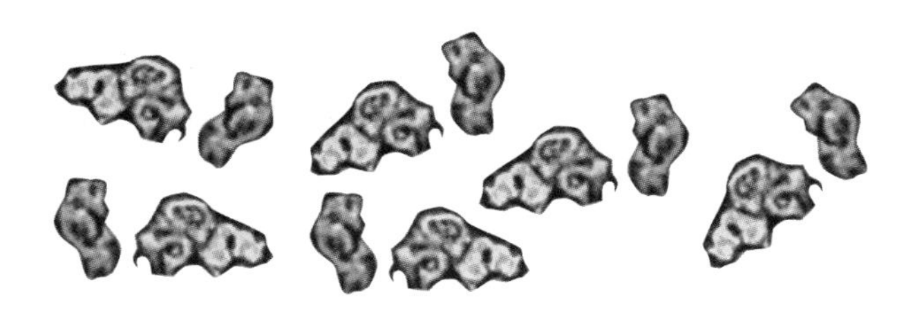

Asparagus

A hardy perennial that needs a permanent site and a lot of patience – seed to plate will take 3 years; even starting with one year old crowns will still take 2 years!

Care:

- ✔ To encourage longer blanched stems, make a ridge (earth up like potatoes), approx 12cm (5") over stems before they appear.
- ✔ Trim stems back when yellow to 5cm (2") in autumn.
- ✔ Flatten ridge when cutting back in autumn.
- ✔ Don't harvest foliage.

Pests: Slugs, Asparagus beetle.
Diseases: Violet root rot, Rust.

Harvesting:

Cut from only 2+ year old plants when spears reach 10-12cm (4-5"). Cut spears approx 7cm (3") below the surface. Cut until mid- June to encourage a good crop next season.

Take care!
Never allow crowns to dry out.

Site	Soil	Comments
	Light and well drained L 2	Shelter and protect from winds

Planting to plate	2-3 years
Expected yield	20 spears

Plants produce well for 10-12 years. Replace old stock as required.

Sowing:

Follow the packet instructions, plant out next spring.

Planting:

It is more reliable to buy/use your own rooted 1 year old male crowns. Dig shallow trenches 20cm (8") deep and lay crowns out on compost 'hills' approx 5cm (2") high. Cover with sifted soil or compost and water in well.

	J		F		M		A		M		J		J		A		S		O		N		D	
Sow						■	■	■																
Plant							■	■																
Eat									■	■	■													

Spacing:

30cm apart x 36cm rows (12 x 15") 15cm (6") deep.

Asparagus Pea

An easy annual crop which is perfect for the ornamental kitchen garden. These unusual plants have a profusion of red flowers and form triangular winged pods; they will happily crop throughout the summer. Plants grow to 45cm (18").

Care:

- ✔ Protect emerging seedlings from pests.
- ✔ Pick regularly to encourage more pods.

Pests: Slugs, rabbits, mice, birds, aphids.

Diseases: Downy/powdery mildew.

Harvesting:

Small pods are best! Pick when 2-3cm (1-1½").
Eat as soon as you can.

Tip: Protect from birds by using: twigs, (criss crossed over the crop), netting, black thread wound around canes over the whole crop or cloches.

Site	Soil	Comments
	Light and well drained L 1-2	Needs aerated and humus rich soil

Approx germination	7-21 days
Planting to plate	12-15 weeks

Sowing:

Sow in individual cells of compost to plant out after both hardening off and frosts or sow directly into a well prepared, pre-watered, flat bottomed seed drill. Firm the soil down gently.

Planting:

	J		F		M		A		M		J		J		A		S		O		N		D	
Sow							■	■	■	■														
Eat												■	■	■	■	■								

Spacing:

5cm apart x 30cm rows (2 x 12") approx 2cm (1") deep.

Aubergine

A tender annual which has lovely showy purple flowers and glossy fruit. Aubergines need warmth and sunshine so they are most successfully grown behind glass.

Care:

- ✔ Pinch out growing tip at approx 23cm (9").
- ✔ Allow only 4-5 fruits to set and develop.
- ✔ If you are growing under glass, mist regularly to encourage fruit to set.
- ✔ Feed frequently (tomato food) when fruit sets.

Pests: Red spider mite, aphids, whitefly.

Harvesting:

Cut once the fruits are 12-15cm (5-6") long and are still glossy.

Growing Outdoors:

If you can provide a very warm, sheltered spot, it is possible to grow aubergines outside. Harden off and plant out under cloches late May in well drained, very fertile soil. Add a general fertilizer of your choice 1 week before planting. Alternatively, place your plant in a container, harden off and leave to grow in a sunny spot.

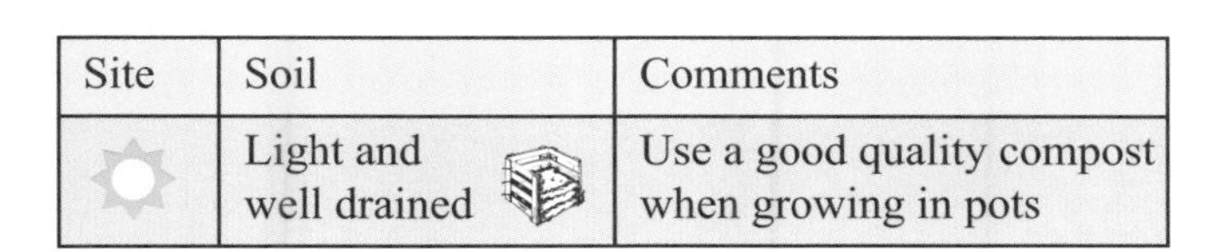

Site	Soil	Comments
	Light and well drained	Use a good quality compost when growing in pots

Approx germination (60 - 70°)	7-21 days
Yield (per mature plant)	4-5 fruits
Planting to plate	20 weeks

Sowing:

Plant 2 seeds to a 7cm (3") pot of compost and keep at 60-70º.

Planting:

When plants are approx 10-13cm (4-5") transplant the stronger plant into final growing area.

	J		F		M		A		M		J		J		A		S		O		N		D	
Sow			■	■	■	■																		
Plant							■	■	■	■														
Eat												■	■	■	■	■	■	■	■					

Spacing:

Pot on into 22cm (9") pots per plant. Alternatively plant 2/3 to a grow bag.

Broad Bean

A hardy annual which is an easily grown and rewarding crop. A standard variety will grow to 90-120cm (3-4ft) and dwarf varieties 30-45cm (12-18").

Care:

- ✔ Remove the top 5cm (2") from plants once pods have begun to set and plenty of flowers remain.
- ✔ Sow successionally to ensure a longer cropping season.

Pests: Slugs, rabbits, mice, birds, black aphids.

Diseases: Chocolate spot, root rot.

Harvesting:

Harvest when the pods begin to bulge and beans show through the pod.

Take care!
Autumn sowings can be disappointing as they are subjected to more extremes. Spring sowings are more reliable and cropping is generally not that far behind earlier winter sowings.

Tip: Very early spring sowings often avoid a serious attack of black aphids as the leaves are just that little bit tougher.

Site	Soil	Comments
	Almost any L 1-2	

Approx germination	7-14 days
Planting to plate (autumn)	26 weeks
Planting to plate (spring)	14-16 weeks

Sowing:

Sow directly into a prepared bed. Taller varieties are usually planted in double rows 20cm apart (8").

Planting:

	J		F		M		A		M		J		J		A		S		O		N		D	
Sow (A)																					■	■		
Sow (S)					■	■	■	■	■															
Eat												■	■	■	■	■	■							

Spacing:

20cm apart x 60cm between rows (8 x 24")
approx 5cm
(2") deep.

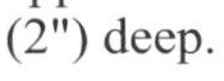

Dwarf/French Bean

A huge array of annual plants that are very easy to grow and need little attention or maintenance. The compact dwarf plants will grow to 45-60cm (1½-2ft) and the climbing varieties 1.8m+ (6ft).

Care:

✔ Sow successionally to ensure a longer cropping season.

Pests: Slugs, rabbits, mice, birds, black fly.

Diseases: Root rot, halo blight.

Harvesting:

To eat: Harvest when the pods are approximately 8cm (3"). Regular picking will ensure a longer cropping season.

To dry: Leave the beans to mature on the plant and then dry thoroughly.

Tip: For an earlier crop try growing in pots, under glass in late April. Harden off and plant out after the last frosts have passed and soil has warmed up.

Site	Soil	Comments
	Almost any L	Avoid windy sites

Approx germination	7-14 days
Planting to plate (spring)	10-12 weeks

Sowing:

Sow directly into shallow trenches in a prepared bed.

Planting:

	J	F	M	A	M	J	J	A	S	O	N	D
Sow												
Eat												

Spacing:

10cm apart x 30-45cm between rows (4 x 12-18") approx 5cm (2") deep.

Runner Bean

A tender perennial, grown annually, the runner bean is one of the most popular home grown vegetables. A wall of bright red flowers is a sure sign of summer. The runner bean plant will easily reach 2.4m (8ft).

Care:

- ✔ A very heavy crop which needs *secure* staking. Lightweight stakes will easily topple over in a wind.
- ✔ Liquid feed occasionally once pods have set.
- ✔ It is best to pinch out growing tips once the plants are too tall to harvest any resulting beans.

Pests: Slugs, rabbits, mice, birds, black fly.

Diseases: Root rot, halo blight.

Harvesting:

Pick when the pods are approximately 20cm (8") and still tender. Regular picking is necessary to ensure a longer cropping season.

Tips: Do not be in a rush to plant out the beans that you have raised under glass. Poor weather will check the young plants growth to the point you may have to start again.

* Keep a few 'spares' to replace the ones eaten by slugs!

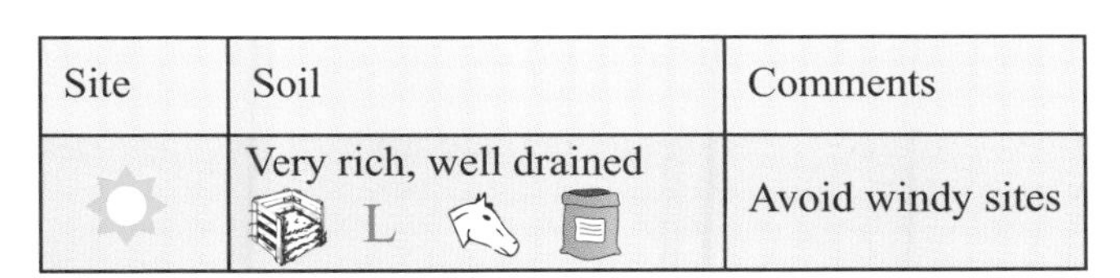

Site	Soil	Comments
	Very rich, well drained L	Avoid windy sites

Approx germination	7-14 days
Planting to plate	12-16 weeks

Sowing:

To get an early start, sow one seed in a 7cm (3") pot, early May, under glass. Harden off before planting out after all risk of frosts or sow directly into shallow trenches in a prepared bed later in the season (early June) when the soil has warmed up.

Planting:

Give each plant a cane of its own and gently tie in/secure onto stake. The plants will wrap themselves around their support once they start to grow.

	J	F	M	A	M	J	J	A	S	O	N	D
Sow					■	■						
Plant						■	■	■	■	■		
Eat							■	■	■	■		

Spacing:

Rows: 20cm apart x 45cm between rows (8 x 18") approx 5cm (2") deep.
Wigwams: Space canes with a 20cm space (8").

Beetroot

There is a huge range of this easy to grow annual root. There are two types - the root or the globe - both are grown in the same way and are best pulled before they get too large and woody.

Care:

- ✔ Thin seedlings when large enough to handle easily approx 2cm (1") high.
- ✔ Don't allow to dry out – roots become woody.

Pests: Slugs, mice, birds, black fly.

Diseases: Leaf miner, downy mildew, leaf spot.

Harvesting:

Beetroots are perfectly usable when they reach 4-5cm (1¾-2"). If you want larger roots, keep thinning until they grow to their full size, normally no larger than a tennis ball!

Tip: * A great plant for successional sowing.
* Leaves from the thinning can be used in salads.

Take care: Beetroot are notorious for bleeding, so twist leaves off leaving 5cm (2") of stalks.

Site	Soil	Comments
	Well drained 1-2	Prefers light, deeply dug soil.

Approx germination	10-20 days
Planting to plate (globe)	12 weeks
Planting to plate (long)	16-18 weeks

Sowing:

Sow very thinly, direct into pre-watered shallow drills in a prepared bed. Firm seeds down gently.

Planting:

	J	F	M	A	M	J	J	A	S	O	N	D
Sow			■■	■■	■■	■■						
Eat						■■	■■	■■	■■			

Spacing:

7cm apart x 30cm between rows (3 x 12") approx 2cm (1") deep.

Broccoli

There are two types of this hardy biennial plant, curding and sprouting. Both are notoriously difficult to grow and are a definite favourite with most pests. Both types are hungry plants that need plenty of space and occupy the ground for a long time, generally reaching up to 1.5m (3½ft).

Care:

Pests: Slugs, mice, birds, black/white fly, mealy aphid, cutworm, flee beetles, chafer grubs, caterpillars.

Diseases: Leaf miner, downy mildew, leaf spot, club root, white rust, wire stem, whiptail.

Harvesting:

Cut the main central head once it has reached a reasonable size and then cut side shoots when they reach 10-12cm (4-5") but always before the individual flower heads have opened.

Site	Soil	Comments
	L 1-2	Soil must be compact

Approx germination	8-14 days
Planting to plate (Summer Calabrese types)	12-14 weeks
Planting to plate (Sprouting/Winter types)	44+ weeks

Sowing:

Grow in prepared beds or individual cells to transplant. Plants need 4-6 true leaves and be at least 10cm (4") before planting out. Water well beforehand and always use a fork/trowel to move seedlings as broccoli are shallow rooted.

Planting:

	J		F		M		A		M		J		J		A		S		O		N		D	
Sow							■	■	■	■														
Plant											■	■	■	■										
Eat			■	■	■	■		■	■						■	■	■	■	■					

Spacing:

45cm apart x 45cm between rows (18" x 18"). Try to plant approx 2cm (1") deeper than root ball.

Brussels Sprouts

A hungry, nitrogen loving, hardy biennial crop. The main challenge for successful sprouts is in the preparation of the soil and planting. Plants grow to approx 90cm (3ft).

Care:

✔ Compost any yellow leaves as they fall.
✔ Keep a watchful eye for pests.

Pests: Slugs, birds, black/white fly, mealy aphid, cutworm, flea beetles, chafer grubs, caterpillars.

Diseases: Leaf miner, downy mildew, leaf spot, club root, white rust, wire stem.

Harvesting:

Harvest (snap off or cut) from the bottom up when sprouts are large enough but are still firmly closed. Some say to always leave a few sprouts on each stalk until completely harvested.

Tip: Before discarding plants completely, use the remaining top leaves as a spring green crop.

Site	Soil	Comments
	L 1-2	Soil must be compact

Approx germination	7-14 days
Planting to plate (early)	30 weeks
Planting to plate (late)	36+ weeks

Sowing:

Grow in prepared beds or individual cells to transplant. Plants need 4-6 true leaves and be at least 10cm (4") before planting. Water well beforehand and always use a fork/trowel to move seedlings.

Planting:

	J		F		M		A		M		J		J		A		S		O		N		D	
Sow						■	■	■																
Plant									■	■	■	■												
Eat	■	■	■	■														■	■	■	■	■	■	■

Spacing:

75cm apart x 75cm between rows (2½ x 2½ft). Plant with the lower leaves approx1cm (½") above the soil surface.

Cabbage

A nitrogen loving biennial plant that has numerous varieties. If you have enough space and choose your varieties carefully, you can grow cabbage almost all year round. Most pests love cabbage so you need to be vigilant.

Care:

✔ Liquid feed occasionally when heads form.

Pests: Slugs, mice, birds, black/white fly, mealy aphid, cutworm, flee beetles, chafer grubs, caterpillars.

Diseases: Leaf miner, downy mildew, leaf spot, club root, white rust, wire stem.

Harvesting:

Cut as needed when the hearts have formed and feel firm to the touch.

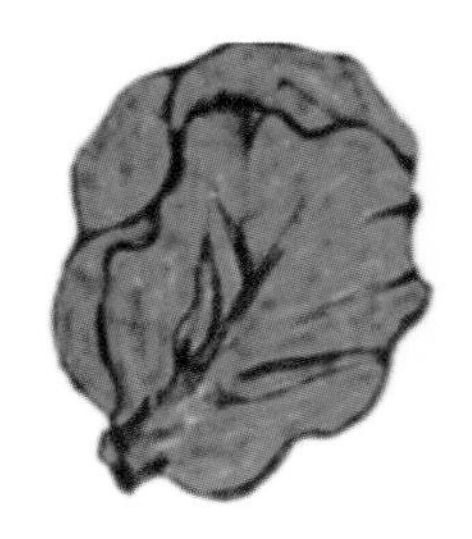

Spacing:

90cm apart x 90cm between rows (18" x 18"). Try to plant approx 2cm (1") deeper than root ball.

Easy ***

Site	Soil	Comments
	L 1-2	Soil must be compact

Approx germination	7-14 days
Planting to plate (Chinese)	10 weeks
Planting to plate (summer/winter)	44+ weeks
Planting to plate (spring)	32 weeks

Sowing:

Grow in prepared beds or individual cells to transplant. Plants need 5-6 true leaves and be at least 10-13cm (4-5") before planting. Water well beforehand and always use a fork/trowel to move seedlings.

Planting:

	J	F	M	A	M	J	J	A	S	O	N	D
Sow												
Plant												
Eat												
	Summer			Spring			Winter/Savoy					

	J	F	M	A	M	J	J	A	S	O	N	D
Sow												
Plant												
Eat												

Carrot

One of those crops that is supposedly easy to grow, but in practice is quite tricky. Carrots are notoriously difficult to germinate and get started, yet once you do, they are an easily maintained crop. Short rooted varieties are faster to mature.

Care:

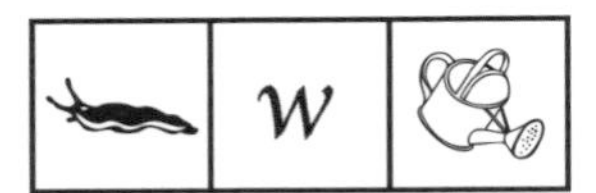

✔ Remember to firm the soil around existing roots once you start thinning and lifting.

Pests: Carrot root fly, slugs

Diseases: Black/Violet root rot.

Ailments: Fanging, splitting, green top.

Harvesting:

Baby carrots from thinnings are very sweet and can be used easily. Lift as required from July onwards.

Tips: Carrot root fly is the dreaded carrot pest! When tending the crop, try snapping off sprigs of mint, bruise/rub between your fingers and then plant round the carrot.

Use fresh seed each year for best results.

Site	Soil		Comments
☀	Well drained, sandy	1-2	Prefers light, deeply dug soil with no stones

Approx germination	14-21 days
Planting to plate (early)	12-14 weeks
Planting to plate (main crop)	16-20 weeks

Sowing:

Sow very thinly, directly into pre-watered shallow drills in a prepared bed. Firm down soil gently. Thin seedlings to approx 4-5cm (2") when they are large enough to handle.

Planting:

Growing carrots off ground level and in containers is often more successful as the carrot root fly is thought to only fly low.

	J		F		M		A		M		J		J		A		S		O		N		D	
Sow						■	■	■	■	■	■	■												
Eat												■	■	■	■	■	■	■	■	■	■			

Spacing:

5cm apart x 15cm between rows (2 x 6") approx 1cm (½") deep.

Cauliflower

A half hardy biennial plant, which is well known as a difficult crop to grow. It is a hungry plant which needs plenty of space. With careful selection of varieties, cauliflowers can be harvested for a long season. Plants grow to approx 60cm (2ft).

Care:

- ✔ Feed occasionally with a liquid feed.
- ✔ Break a few leaves over the developing curds to protect from both sun and frost.

Pests: Slugs, birds, cabbage root, black/white fly, flea beetles, caterpillars.

Diseases: Downy mildew, leaf spot, club root wire stem, whiptail.

Harvesting:

Cut the head once it has reached a reasonable size but always before the individual flower heads have opened.

Beware! Rabbits love cauliflower leaves if they can get them.

Site	Soil	Comments
	L 1-2	Soil must be compact

Approx germination	7-14 days
Planting to plate (summer/autumn types)	20-24 weeks
Planting to plate (winter types)	45-50 weeks

Sowing:

Grow in prepared beds or individual cells to transplant. Plants need 4-6 true leaves and be at least 10cm (4") before planting. Water well beforehand and always use a fork/trowel to move as cauliflower seedlings particularly dislike any root disturbance.

Planting:

	J	F	M	A	M	J	J	A	S	O	N	D
Sow				■ ■	■ ■							
Plant						■ ■	■ ■					
Eat			■ ■	■ ■	■ ■	░ ░	░ ░	░	■	■ ■	■ ■	

■ Winter ░ Summer ■ Autumn

Spacing:

60cm apart x 60cm between rows (2ft x 2ft). Try to plant a little deeper than root base from seed bed.

.

Celeriac

A hardy biennial plant that is grown as an annual for both its root and leaves. Celeriac is an easy vegetable to grow and has a mild celery taste. Plants grow to approx 45cm (1½ft).

Care:

- ✔ Protect young plants from frost until established.
- ✔ Feed occasionally with a liquid feed.
- ✔ Remove any side shoots as they grow.
- ✔ From August onwards, start to remove a few of the bottom leaves to help root ripen.
- ✔ If you intend to keep in the ground for a few weeks, make sure there is soil around the root to protect from both sun and frost.

Pests: Slugs, carrot and celery root fly.

Diseases: Celery leaf spot, mosaic virus, damping off.

Harvesting:

Lift as required from October onwards. Celeriac will keep growing and larger roots will be available from November onwards.

Site	Soil	Comments
	1-2	Prefers moisture retentive soil

Approx germination (70°)	14-21 days
Planting to plate (summer/autumn types)	20+ weeks

Sowing:

Grow under glass in individual 9cm pots (3½"). Prick out when large enough to handle. When plants reach 10-12cm (4-5") harden off before planting out into final position.

Planting:

	J		F		M		A		M		J		J		A		S		O		N		D	
Sow					■	■																		
Plant										■	■													
Eat																			■	■	■	■	■	■

Spacing:

30cm apart x 45cm between rows (12 x18").

Plant firmly but do not cover crown.

Celery

A hardy biennial plant, grown as an annual. For ease, choose the self blanching types as the traditional are labour intensive and time consuming. Plants can grow to approx 45cm (18").

Care:

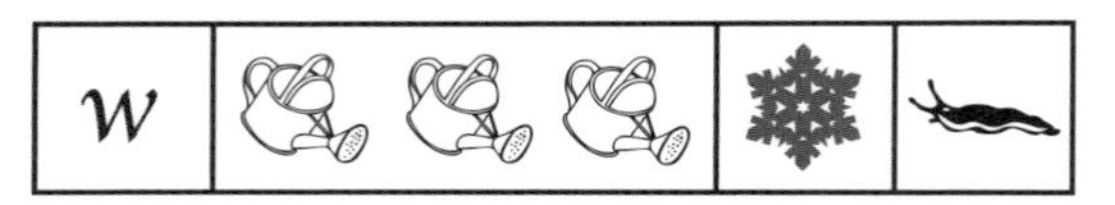

✔ Feed occasionally with a liquid feed.
✔ Do not allow the celery to dry out, it needs water.

Additional instructions for traditional types: Dig a 30cm deep trench, half fill with a layer of compost/manure and then fill to top with soil. When stalks reach approx 30 cm (1ft) loosely wrap newspaper/soft cardboard around stalks and fill this tube up to the top (in stages as the plant grows) with compost.

Pests: Slugs, carrot and celery root fly.

Diseases: Celery leaf spot, mosaic virus, damping off, celery heart.

Harvesting:

Self blanching: Lift anytime after August. Harvest before frosts.

Traditional: Lift when ready anytime after end of September. Usually 8-10 weeks after blanching begins.

Tip: If you plant seedlings in blocks, some shade is provided which will be useful for both types.

*Easy(Self Blanching)*** *Easy(Traditional)******

Site	Soil	Comments
	1-2	Prefers moisture retentive soil

Approx germination (70°)	14-21 days
Planting to plate (Self Blanching)	22+ weeks
Planting to plate (Traditional)	35+ weeks

Sowing:

Grow under glass in cells or individual 9cm pots (3½"). Prick out when large enough to handle and grow on. When plants reach 10-12cm (4-5") harden off before planting out into final position.

Planting:

	J		F		M		A		M		J		J		A		S		O		N		D	
Sow					■	■																		
Plant										■	■													
Eat																			■	■	■	■	■	■

Spacing:

Self blanching: 20cm apart x 30cm between rows (9x12").
Traditional: In trenches, 25cm x40cm (10x15").
Plant firmly at crown level.

Chard (Swiss Chard/Spinach Beet)

A hardy biennial plant, grown as an annual, that once established will tolerate both heat and frost. The main challenge is creating a soil rich in organic matter to sustain rapid growth. Sow in spring for a summer crop and in summer for a winter crop. Plants can grow to approx 30cm (12").

Care:

- ✔ For overwintering plants, provide light protection from frost (fleece is ideal).
- ✔ Thin seedlings regularly.

Pests: Slugs, mangold fly.

Diseases: Leaf spot, cucumber mosaic virus (spinach blight), damping off, downy mildew.

Harvesting:

Start to pick/cut the outer leaves as soon as they are big enough. The more you pick the more you'll grow!

Tip: In a hot summer, to help prevent bolting, plants may benefit from light shade.

Site	Soil	Comments
	L 1-2	Prefers moisture retentive soil

Approx germination	10-16 days
Planting to plate	8+ weeks

Sowing:

Sow in trays ready to plant out when seedlings reach 5-7cm (2-3") or sow thinly direct into prepared bed.

Planting:

A crop for successional sowing.

	J	F	M	A	M	J	J	A	S	O	N	D
Sow												
Eat												
	Winter			Summer								

Spacing:

15cm apart x 30cm between rows (6 x12") 2cm (1") deep.

Chicory

There are two types of chicory. The forced 'chicon' type is a hardy perennial grown as an annual. The roots are developed and then lifted for forcing later in the season. The half hardy annual radicchio type is grown in summer.

Care:

- ✔ Once established, keep reasonably dry to encourage root growth for forcing types.
- ✔ Liquid feed once or twice to aid leaf production.

Pests:

Slugs, cutworm, wireworm.

Harvesting:

Forcing: Dig up, using a fork, late autumn and cut the leaves off just above the crown, trim roots to 30cm (12") and store in sand in a frost-free shed.

Radicchio: Cut heads as required when large enough.

Forcing:

Force a few at a time when needed in winter. Plant 4-5 in a large pot of moist compost with the crowns just showing, keep above 10° and cover with a bucket to exclude the light. Chicons should be ready within 3-4 weeks. A smaller chicon should follow after the first cutting.

Site	Soil	Comments
☼	L 1	Prefers fertile, light well drained soil

Approx germination	7-14 days
Planting to plate	20-32 weeks

Sowing:

Sow directly into prepared drills 1cm (½") deep where plants are to grow, thin seedlings to 23cm (9") forcing, 30cm (12") radicchio.

Planting:

F - Forcing **R** - Radicchio

	J		F		M		A		M		J		J		A		S		O		N		D	
Sow F									■	■	■													
Cut F	■	■	■	■	■																		■	■
Sow R											■	■	■											
Cut R																		■	■	■	■	■	■	■

Spacing:

30cm apart x 30cm between rows (12 x 12") 1cm (½") deep.

Chinese Artichoke

An unusually shaped, perennial tuber, that belongs to the mint family and is grown as an annual crop. The plant has pretty pink flowers and the tubers have a nutty taste with a texture like water chestnuts. A crop that, once established, will tolerate both high temperatures and frost. Plants will grow to approx 45cm (18").

Care:

- ✔ Avoid frost on leaves when first planted.
- ✔ Keep well watered as tubers are developing.
- ✔ Give an occasional liquid feed.
- ✔ Earth up when plants reach 30cm (12").

Pests: Earwigs, aphids, slugs, snails.

Diseases: Mosaic virus.

Harvesting:

As soon as the leaves die down, dig up and use when needed because the tubers soon dry out and wither. The tubers are produced on 'strings' and should be approx 5cm (2") long and 1.5cm (¾") wide.

Beware: Remove all tubers because this can be an invasive crop. They will come back next year!

Tip: Try growing a few in a grow bag.

Site	Soil	Comments
	1-2	Needs free draining soil

Approx germination	14-21 days
Planting to plate	8 weeks

Sowing:

Soil needs to have reached 10° before planting directly into a prepared bed 2-5cm (1-2") deep.

Planting:

	J	F	M	A	M	J	J	A	S	O	N	D
Sow F			■	■								
Cut F	■	■									■	■

Spacing:

22cm apart x 45cm between rows (9 x 18") 2-5cm (1-2") deep.

Corn Sald (Lambs Lettuce)

A hardy annual crop that is easy to grow. Best grown as an autumn/winter crop, it has a mild taste and is a welcome addition when there are very few salad crops available. There are two main types, the smaller dark green leaved and the larger light green leaved. Plants will grow to approx 15-25cm (6-10").

Care:

- ✔ Weed carefully by hand.
- ✔ Give some cloche protection over winter to encourage growth.

Pests: Generally pest free.

Diseases: Generally disease free.

Harvesting:

Once the plants have developed 3-4 sets of leaves, usually little rosettes of approx 2-5cm (1-2"), pick as needed by pinching out the tips. Never strip a plant bare.

Tip: The larger type is easier to harvest.

Site	Soil	Comments
	1-2	Needs nitrogen rich, free draining soil

Approx germination	14-21 days
Planting to plate	8 weeks

Sowing:

Either sow seeds in trays for transplanting or sow seeds thinly 1cm (½") deep in prepared drills.

Planting:

	J	F	M	A	M	J	J	A	S	O	N	D
Sow			░░	░░				■■	■■			
Eat	■■	■■								■■	■■	■■

■ Winter ░ Summer

Spacing:

10cm apart x 15cm between rows (4 x 6") 1cm deep.

Cucumber (Indoor)

A half hardy annual that needs warmth and sunshine so they are only grown behind glass. Even then, they are a reasonably difficult crop to grow successfully. Beginners may have more success with the outdoor type. Indoor plants will climb until stopped.

Care:

- ✔ Minimum temperature 65-70°.
- ✔ Pinch out growing tip when it reaches top of green house.
- ✔ Pinch out side shoots after 2 true sets of leaves develop, after the flower, (only keep female flowers; they will have a mini cucumber already forming behind the flower).
- ✔ Raise humidity by watering floor.
- ✔ Feed frequently (tomato food) when fruit sets.

Pests: Red spider mite, aphids, whitefly.

Diseases: Cucumber mosaic virus, grey mould, gummosis, sclerotinia rot, black rot, leaf spot, basal/stem rot.

Harvesting:

Cut when fruits reach a reasonable size, approx 15-23cm. (6-9") Regular picking encourages more cropping.

Site	Soil	Comments
	Compost/Grow bags	Use a good quality compost when growing in pots

Approx germination (70-80°)	5-7 days
Yield (per mature plant)	10-15 fruits
Planting to plate	15 weeks

Sowing:

Plant 2 seeds (edgeways) to a 7cm (3") pot of compost and keep at 60-70°. Remove weaker seedling.

Planting:

Guidance given for heated ▼ and unheated ▽ greenhouses

	J		F		M		A		M		J		J		A		S		O		N		D	
Sow				▼	▼	▼		▽	▽															
Plant						▼	▼				▽													
Eat												■	■	■	■	■	■	■						

Spacing:

Pot on into 22cm (9") pots per plant, alternatively plant 2 to a grow bag.

Beware: If a cucumber is left to set seed, cropping will stop.

Cucumber (Outdoor)

A half hardy annual that needs warmth and sunshine. The easier of the cucumbers to grow but still fiddly and time consuming.

Care:

- ✔ Pinch out growing tip after 8 leaves to encourage bushy growth.
- ✔ Feed frequently (tomato food) when fruit sets.

Pests: Red spider mite, aphids, whitefly.

Diseases: Cucumber mosaic virus, grey mould, gummosis, sclerotinia rot, black rot, leaf spot, basal/stem rot.

Harvesting:

Cut when fruits reach a reasonable size, usually 15cm (6"). Regular picking encourages more cropping.

Beware: If a cucumber is left to set seed cropping will stop.

Tip: Bury a couple of 10cm (4") plant pots next to the plant and fill with water.

Site	Soil	Comments
	1-2	Prefers well drained soil

Approx germination (70-80°)	7-10 days
Yield (per mature plant)	5-8 fruits
Planting to plate	15+ weeks

Sowing:

Plant 2 seeds (edgeways) to a 7cm (3") pot of compost and keep at 70-80º. Remove weaker seedling before hardening off prior to planting out. Alternatively, plant out directly and protect seedlings with a cloche until established.

Planting:

Prepare a hole approx 30cm (12") deep and fill with compost/manure ready for either the seed or plant.

	J		F		M		A		M		J		J		A		S		O		N		D	
Sow							■			■	■													
Eat															■	■	■							

Spacing:

15 cm apart x 30cm between rows (12 x 18") 2cm (1") deep.

Endive

A half hardy annual that resembles a lettuce with lots of leaves. The main challenge for successful endives is creating a soil rich in organic matter to sustain rapid growth.

Care:

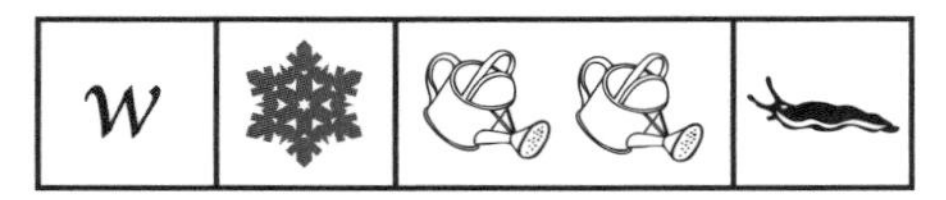

- ✔ Thin seedlings as soon as they are large enough to handle, Keep thinning until they are approx 30 cm (12") apart.
- ✔ Liquid feed once or twice to aid leaf production.

Pests: Slugs, aphids.

Blanching:

Approximately 12 weeks after sowing the seed, either: gather the leaves together when dry and tie as many of the central leaves with raffia to exclude the light or, just place something like a large pot over the top of the plant. The only requirement is to ensure no light gets to the leaves. (Not such pretty results but faster and easier!)

Harvesting:

Cut the whole plant when blanching is finished approx 7-10 days summer/3 weeks autumn. Start the blanching process on just a few endives at a time as they do not keep very well after blanching.

Easy ****

Site	Soil	Comments
	 1-2	Prefers light, well drained soil

Approx germination	5-8 days
Planting to plate	14+ weeks

Sowing:

Sow directly where plants are to grow - avoid root disturbance.

Planting:

A good crop for successional sowing, it is possible to harvest endive for 6 months of the year.

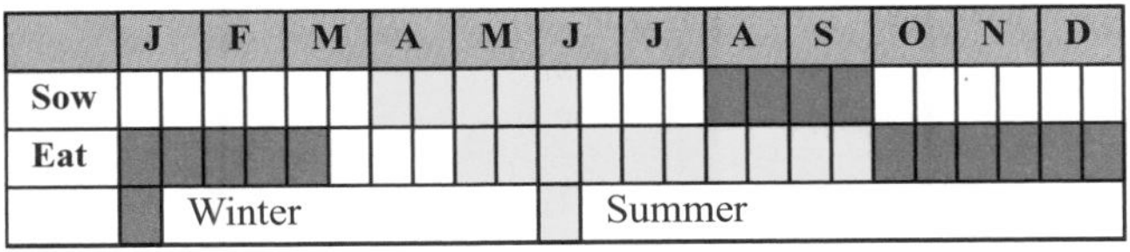

	J	F	M	A	M	J	J	A	S	O	N	D
Sow												
Eat												
	Winter					Summer						

Spacing:

30cm apart x 30cm between rows (12 x 12") 1cm (½") deep.

Tip: In a hot summer, to help prevent bolting, plants may benefit from light shade and plenty of moisture.

Florence Fennel

An annual plant, which is a dwarf variety of the common fennel. Grown for its aniseed flavoured bulbs it is very fast and easy to grow. Plants will reach 90cm (3ft) at least.

Care:

W			

✔ Plant out late June to prevent bolting.
✔ Keep well watered as the bulb is developing.
✔ Liquid feed once or twice to aid leaf production.
✔ Earth up around bulbs to improve sweetness.
✔ Cut out any flower stems that form.

Pests: Slugs.

Diseases: Generally disease free.

Harvesting:

The fennel bulbs can be used as soon as they are large enough. To prevent any damage use a large fork when lifting.

Tip: Florence fennel is a Mediterranean Plant. By delaying planting out into mid-late June the plant has a better start and should not have its growth delayed by cool weather.

Site	Soil	Comments
	1-2	Prefers light, sandy well drained soil

Approx germination (50-60°)	14-21 days
Planting to plate	14-16 weeks

Sowing:

Either: Sow into individual cells or pots of compost, prick out into 13cm (5") pots and grow on. Harden off before planting out in mid/late June *or* Sow seeds thinly 1cm (½") deep from May to July in prepared drills. Thin the seedlings when large enough to handle.

Planting:

	J		F		M		A		M		J		J		A		S		O		N		D	
Sow							pot	pot	pot	■	■	■	■											
Plant												■	■											
Eat														■	■	■	■	■	■	■				

Spacing:

45cm apart x 30cm between rows (18 x 12") 1cm (½") deep.

Hamburg Parsley

An unusual but easy to maintain hardy perennial root crop. The root looks like a parsnip but has a slight celery taste and the leaves can be used as parsley. Plants will grow to approx 37-45cm (15-18").

Care:

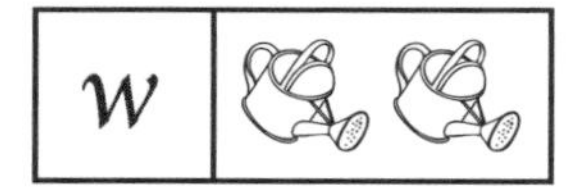

- ✔ Weed by hand, do not disturb crowns.
- ✔ Mulch to conserve moisture. Hamburg Parsley will split/fork if allowed to dry out.

Pests: Generally pest free.

Diseases: Parsnip canker.

Harvesting:

The roots should be ready from late August.

Roots reach approx 20cm (8"). Lift using a fork when needed. These roots will happily overwinter in the ground. It is said that their taste improves with frost.

Tip: Use fresh seed for best results.

Site	Soil	Comments
	1-2	Needs deeply dug, free draining soil

Approx germination	12+ days erratic & slow
Planting to plate	26+ weeks

Sowing:

Hamburg Parsley is notoriously difficult to germinate Either: Sow 3 seeds to one station in a prepared seed drill approx 1cm (½) deep, removing the weakest, thin to approx 15cm (6") or sow in pots ready to transplant out into previously well watered rows when just large enough to handle.

Planting:

	J	F	M	A	M	J	J	A	S	O	N	D
Sow			■	■				■				
Eat	■	■	■						■	■	■	■

Spacing:

15cm apart x 24cm between rows (6 x 9") 1cm (½") deep.

Horseradish

A hardy perennial, which is grown in the same spot to form a clump. This easy to grow peppery tasting plant has pretty, white fragrant flowers. If left unchecked horseradish roots will quickly invade a large space – far more than one family can eat! Plants can easily grow to 90cm (3ft).

Care:

✔ Weed by hand, do not disturb crowns.

Diseases: Mosaic virus, leaf spot, white blister.

Harvesting:

The roots, which can easily grow to 60cm (2ft), should be ready from late August.

Tip: The peppery leaves can be used raw – small are best.

Site	Soil	Comments
	1-2	Prefers rich stone free sandy soil

Approx germination	14-24 days
Planting to plate	32+ weeks

Sowing:

Buy roots (known as thongs) and plant vertically so as top of thong is approx 8cm (3") below the soil surface.

Planting:

	J	F	M	A	M	J	J	A	S	O	N	D
Sow			■									
Eat								■	■	■		

Spacing:

30cm apart x 45cm between rows (12 x 18") 8cm (3") below the soil surface.

Kale (Borecole)

A hardy biennial crop, which is grown as an annual. There are two main varieties, curled or plain leaved. Kale is the easiest and most reliable type of brassica to grow and will reward you with a sustained crop from late summer through to spring. Depending upon variety, plants can grow to approx 100cm (3½ft).

Care:

- ✔ Make sure ground is kept firm around stems.
- ✔ Liquid feed occasionally to maintain healthy growth.

Pests: Slugs, birds, white fly, mealy aphid, flea beetles, caterpillars.

Diseases: Violet root rot, wire stem, damping off.

Harvesting:

Either harvest the leaves (snap off or cut) from the centre of each plant to encourage growth of side shoots which will give you a longer cropping season or, just take the lower leaves as they grow large enough to use.

Tip: Green dwarf curled is a reliable choice, easy to grow and mainly trouble free - even the seedlings are easy to raise.

Site	Soil	Comments
	1-2 L	Soil must be compact but well drained

Approx germination	7-14 days
Planting to plate (fast growing dwarf)	14+ fruits
Planting to plate (traditional)	30+ weeks

Sowing:

Grow in prepared beds or individual cells to transplant. Plants need 4-6 true leaves and should be at least 10cm (4") before planting out. Water well beforehand and always use a fork/trowel to move from the seed bed.

Planting:

	J		F		M		A		M		J		J		A		S		O		N		D	
Sow								■	■	■														
Plant											■	■												
Eat	■	■	■	■	■	■	■											■	■	■	■	■	■	■

Spacing:

60cm apart x 60cm between rows (2 x 2 ft).
Dwarf varieties: 45cm x 45cm (18" x 18"). Plant with the lower leaves approx1cm (½") above the soil surface.

Kohl Rabi

A biennial crop, grown as an annual, that is a really easy and unusual vegetable to grow. It has a mild taste, similar to that of a broccoli stem. Plants grow to approx 30cm (1ft).

Care:

✔ Liquid feed occasionally to maintain healthy growth.

Pests: Slugs, white fly.

Diseases: Club root.

Harvesting:

Kohl rabi are best when eaten small and sweet. The larger they grow, the more woody they become. Lift the roots when about the size of a tennis ball.

Tips:
* Useful as a catch crop
* Kohl rabi do not store very well so for a sustained crop sow at 3 weekly intervals.

Site	Soil	Comments
	1-2 L	Prefers well drained soil

Approx germination	10-14 days
Planting to plate	10+ weeks

Sowing:

Either: Grow in prepared beds of shallow drills 1cm (½") deep and thin regularly once seedlings are large enough to handle or sow in individual cells to transplant (plants need 4 true leaves before transplanting). Water well beforehand and always use a fork/trowel to move from the seed bed.

Planting:

	J	F	M	A	M	J	J	A	S	O	N	D
Sow												
Eat												

Spacing:

15cm apart x 30cm between rows (6" x 12).

Leek

A hardy biennial that is an easy vegetable to grow but does take up the ground for a long time. By growing some of each of the three main varieties (early, mid-season and late) you can harvest leeks over a long period of time. Plants grow to approx 45cm + (1½ft).

Care:

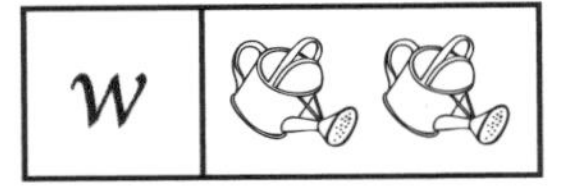

✔ Liquid feed occasionally to maintain strong and healthygrowth (not after September).

Pests: Onion fly.

Diseases: White rot, rust.

Planting:

Trench: (*Leeks will have longer blanched stems*) Dig trenches 30cm (12") deep and wide. Add 10-12cm (4-5") of well rotted manure/compost and plant seedlings approx 2cm (1") deep in the bottom. 4-5 weeks after planting start to fill trenches with the soil previously dug out. Continue this process, (probablymonthly) until the soil is level.

Holes: (*Shorter thicker blanched stems*) Using a dibber, make a 15cm (6") deep hole, drop in the seedling and water in well to 'settle the roots'.

Harvesting:

Lift when needed after the plants reach a size worth eating!

Site	Soil	Comments
	1-2	Prefers rich well drained soil

Approx germination	14-21 days
Planting to plate (early types)	30+ weeks
Planting to plate (late types)	42+ weeks

Sowing:

Either: Sow in prepared beds of shallow drills 1cm (½") deep and thin to approx 2cm (1") or sow into **deep** cells. Transplant seedlings when they are approx 15cm tall (6") and reach the thickness of a pencil. Water well before moving.

Planting:

	J	F	M	A	M	J	J	A	S	O	N	D
Sow												
Plant												
Eat												

Spacing:

15-20cm apart x 37cm between rows (6-9" x 15").

Lettuce (Salad leaves)

A half hardy annual that is a fast and easy vegetable to grow, especially the little gem types. With careful sowing and pampering, you can harvest lettuce over a long season. Very low growing plants.

Care:

✔ Do not allow plants to dry out. Leaves will become tough and more prone to bolting.

Pests: Aphid, slugs, root aphid.

Diseases: Downy mildew, grey mould, lettuce virus.

Harvesting:

Lettuce: Lift when a reasonable sized heart has formed.
Leaves: As and when you need them.

Beware: In hot weather, lettuce has a tendency to bolt and seeds are more difficult to germinate. The easiest solution is to plant summer crops in partial shade.

Site	Soil	Comments
	1-2 L	Prefers well drained soil

Approx germination	7-14 days
Planting to plate (early types)	6+ weeks
Planting to plate (late types)	9+ weeks

Sowing:

Either: Sow in small pots of compost ready to transplant (Seedlings need to be a sturdy 4cm (2") or directly in prepared beds of shallow drills 1cm (½") deep and keep thinning until they are spaced 30cm (12") apart.

Planting:

	J	F	M	A	M	J	J	A	S	O	N	D
Sow												
Eat												
	Winter					Summer						

Spacing:

15-20cm apart x 37cm between rows (6-9" x 15").

Tom Thumb varieties need less space.

Mange Touts (Sugar snap)

An easy to grow annual crop with several different varieties that are all cultivated in the same way. The main problem with pea type plants is that most pests love them, hence much effort is used in protecting them. Depending upon variety, these plants grow to 150cm (5ft).

Care:

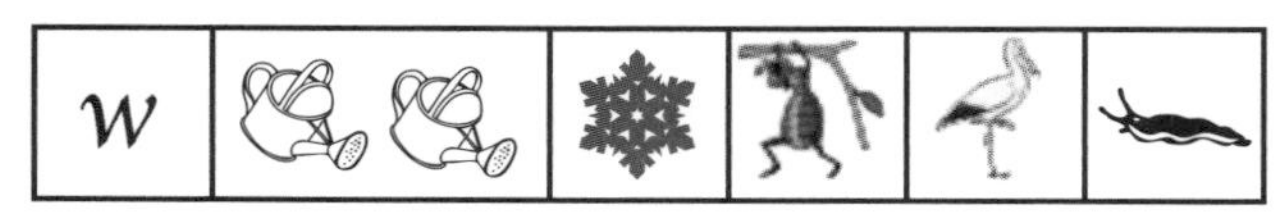

- ✔ Once seeds start to grow, insert twigs or canes in a 'V' shape each side of the row to support the scrambling plants. Tall growing types will need even more support. Netting is ideal.
- ✔ A thick mulch is useful to both conserve moisture round the roots and suppress any weeds.
- ✔ Pick regularly to encourage more pods.

Pests: Slugs, rabbits, mice, aphids, millipedes, weevils.

Diseases: Downy/powdery mildew, damping off, foot/root rot, grey mould, virus diseases.

Harvesting:

Pick when the pods are approx 5-8cm (2-3").

Site	Soil	Comments
	L 1	Needs humus rich soil

Approx germination	7-10 days
Planting to plate	12+ weeks

Sowing:

Prepare a seed drill 15cm wide x 5cm (6 x 2") deep. Water and then sow one seed either side of each edge, refill the trench with soil/compost and firm down.

Planting:

	J		F		M		A		M		J		J		A		S		O		N		D	
Sow							■	■	■	■														
Eat														■	■	■	■							

Spacing:

15cm apart x rows spaced the estimated height of crop (6" x 24"- 5ft) approx 5cm (2") deep.

Tip: Petit pois are best grown in the same way as mange tout and sugar snap peas.

Marrow (Courgette)

A half hardy annual which can trail or form a bush. This plant takes up a lot of space but with a little care will reward you with masses of produce – it is not unusual for one plant to yield 15 courgettes! Depending upon the variety, plants can grow to approx 60cm (2ft) and trail until stopped.

Care:

- ✔ Make sure the ground is kept moist. Bury a couple of empty plant pots, which are easily filled with water, near the roots to make watering easier and more effective.
- ✔ Nip out the growing shoot of trailing types when approx 45cm (18") to encourage the formation of female flowers.
- ✔ Once the fruits start to form, give a liquid feed at least fortnightly to maintain heavy cropping.
- ✔ Lay marrows on straw etc. to keep off the ground to both deter slugs/snails and reduce the risk of rot.

Diseases: Mosaic virus, grey mould, mildew.

Harvesting:

Courgettes are cut once they are approx 12cm (5"+).
Marrows are left to grow to approx 26cm (10").

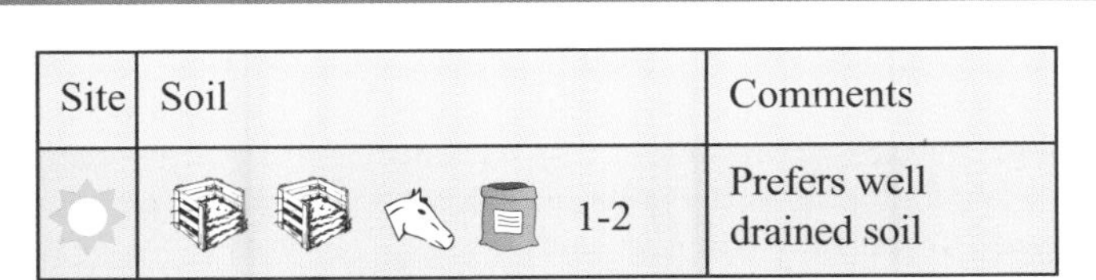

Site	Soil	Comments
	1-2	Prefers well drained soil

Approx germination	5-10 days
Planting to plate (early types)	12+ weeks
Planting to plate (late types)	13+ weeks

Sowing:

Either start off early under glass, 2 seeds, sown edgeways, to a 3" pot. Remove weaker seedling and harden off before planting out or plant 2 seeds to one station, 2cm (1") deep directly into a prepared hole later in the season and remove the weaker seedling.

Planting:

S - Seed

	J		F		M		A		M		J		J		A		S		O		N		D	
Sow								■			S													
Plant										■	■													
Eat												■	■	■	■	■	■	■	■					

Spacing:

Bush: 90cm apart x 90cm between rows (3 x 3 ft).
Trailing: 90cm apart x 150cm between rows (3 x 5ft).

Tip: A mulch of grass clippings early summer helps keep the roots warm and conserves water.

Okra

A tropical tender annual with showy, hibiscus like flowers. Okra needs warmth and sunshine to grow well, so plants are generally more successful when grown behind glass. A constant soil temperature of 65° is required. Plants can reach approx 1.8 -2.4m (6-8ft).

Care:

- ✔ Keep moist, overwatering will encourage stem rot.
- ✔ Keep well supported with a cane.
- ✔ Feed occasionally (high potash content) when fruit sets not before as Okra does not like to be over fertilized.

Pests: Red spider mite, aphids, whitefly, shield bugs.

Diseases: Verticillium/fusarium wilt.

Harvesting:

Pick the long green pods when approx 5-8cm (2-3") long, usually 4-5 days after flowering. Older pods will be tough and stringy. Pick regularly to encourage more pods as Okra will stop producing if existing pods are left too long.

Beware: Okra plants have small spines that can irritate the skin.

Tip: Buy fresh seed each year, Okra seeds do not store very well.

Site	Soil	Comments
☼	Compost	Use good quality compost when growing in pots

Approx germination (60-70°)	5-25 days (heat dependent)
Planting to plate	14 weeks

Sowing:

Soak the seeds overnight to encourage successful germination. Sow the seeds in a pot of compost 2cm (1") deep and keep at a constant 65-70 ° (minimum). As soon as 2 pairs of sturdy leaves have developed, prick out into individual 7cm (3") pots and grow on, still in the warmth. Re pot into a 13cm (5") pot when you can see the roots at the bottom and then again into either a final 23cm (9") pot or directly into the greenhouse border.

Planting:

	J		F		M		A		M		J		J		A		S		O		N		D	
Sow									■	■														
Plant												■												
Eat															■	■	■	■	■					

Spacing:

Pot on into 22cm (9") pots per plant. Alternatively plant 60cm apart in the greenhouse border.

Onions (and Shallots)

A hardy biennial grown as an annual. Onions can be grown from either sets or seeds. Sets are easier, less fiddly and more reliable but you normally get bigger bulbs from seeds even though they are more demanding. Plants will grow to approx 30-45cm (12-18"). For shallots, follow instructions for onion sets.

Care:

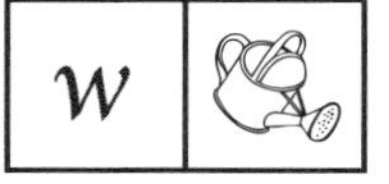

- ✔ Weed by hand, pushing back into the soil any lifted sets.
- ✔ Liquid feed occasionally.
- ✔ Stop watering once bulbs begin to ripen.
- ✔ Nip off any flower stems which may develop.

Pests: Onion fly, cutworm, eelworm, wireworm.

Diseases: Downy mildew, onion smut, rust, soft rot.

Harvesting:

Harvest once the leaves have turned yellow and died down. Leave on the top of soil in full sun for 3-4 weeks to dry off, turning weekly.

Tip: Dry off on slatted shelves in a greenhouse or put harvested onions under cloches to keep dry whilst drying off. Use onions that have bolted first; they do not keep.

Easy (Sets) * *Easy (Seeds)* ***

Site	Soil	Comments
	1-2 L	Prefers well drained soil

Approx germination (sets)/(seeds)	10-14 /18-21 days
Planting to plate (sets and shallots)	20+ weeks
Planting to plate (spring sown seeds)	20+ weeks
Planting to plate (summer sown seeds)	44+ weeks

Sowing:

Sets: Plant with tip just showing directly into the prepared bed. *Seeds*: Sow thinly in prepared drills, keep thinning until 10cm 4" apart. Alternatively sow in deep trays, ready to transplant when seedlings reach approx 8cm (3").

Planting:

	J	F	M	A	M	J	J	A	S	O	N	D
Sow sets												
Sow seed												
Eat sets												
Eat seed												

Spacing:

Sets: 10cm apart x 30cm between rows (4 x 12") tip showing.
Seed: 15cm apart x 30cm between rows (6 x 12") 1cm (½") deep.

Pak Choi (Oriental Vegetables)

A half hardy annual that is a fast, easy and versatile vegetable to grow. A great crop for both intercropping and successional sowing giving a surprisingly long growing season, which can be further extended with a cloche/cold frame. Low growing plants.

Care:

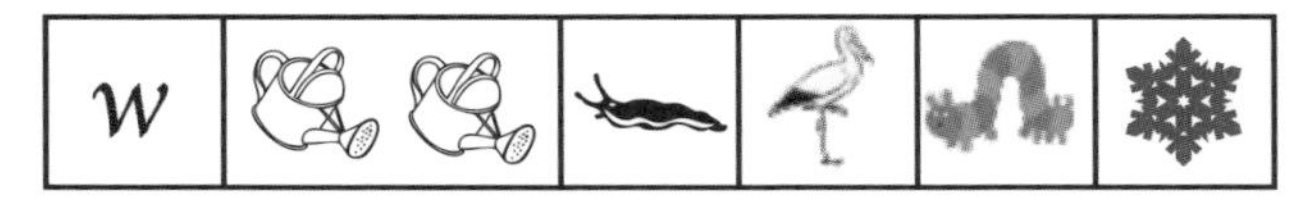

- ✔ Do not allow plants to dry out; plants will be more prone to bolting.
- ✔ Liquid feed weekly.
- ✔ Protect later crops with a cloche/cold frame.

Pests: Aphids, slugs, whitefly, flea beetles.

Diseases: Generally disease free.

Harvesting:

Pak Choi can be grown as a cut and grow again salad type leafcrop or left to become a mature plant. As a leaf crop, pick leaves once the plant has reached 5+cm (2+") or leave until plant reaches approx 15cm (6").

The availability of Oriental vegetable seeds is increasing rapidly. They are all reasonably fast to grow, easy to care for and follow same general rules for Pak Choi.

Site	Soil	Comments
	L 1-2	Prefers well drained soil

Approx germination	7-10 days
Planting to plate (loose leaves/salad types)	4+ weeks
Planting to plate (mature plants)	6+ weeks

Sowing:

Either: Sow in small pots of compost ready to transplant (Seedlings need to be a sturdy 3cm (1") or directly in prepared beds of shallow drills 1cm (½") deep and keep thinning until they are spaced 13cm (5") apart.

Planting:

Check seed packet for specific instructions
but generally the following can be used.

	J		F		M		A		M		J		J		A		S		O		N		D	
Sow						■	■	■	■	■	■	■	■	■	■									
Eat										■	■	■	■	■	■	■	■	■	■					

Spacing:

13cm apart x 30cm between rows (5 x 12") 1cm (½") deep.

Parsnip

A hardy biennial root grown as an annual, Parsnips are notoriously difficult to germinate but once you have germinated seed, the crop needs little care and will fill the ground for a long time. Plants will grow to approx 37-45cm (15-18").

Care:

- ✔ Weed by hand when seedlings are young.
- ✔ Parsnips need watering only in dry spells.

Pests: Celery fly.

Diseases: Parsnip canker.

Harvesting:

Harvest with a fork when needed once leaves have turned yellow and died down. Parsnips will usually overwinter in the ground. In fact, frost is said to improve the taste.

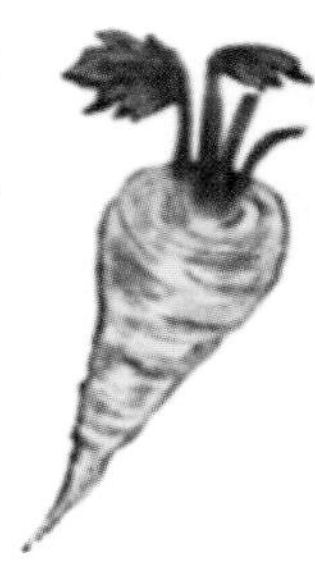

Tip: Parsnip seeds do not store very well. It is best to use fresh seed each year.

Site	Soil	Comments
(sun/partial shade icons)	(compost, manure, fertiliser icons) 1-2 L	Prefers deeply dug, well drained soil

Approx germination	12-30 days
Planting to plate	35+ weeks

Sowing:

The time honoured traditional way states to sow in prepared drills, 1cm deep and then thin to 15cm (6") apart. However, I have had most success with starting the seeds off in pots and carefully transplanting into their well watered, final growing position as soon as they can be handled, (no larger than 1cm).

Planting:

	J	F	M	A	M	J	J	A	S	O	N	D
Sow	□□	□■	■■	□□	□□	□□	□□	□□	□□	□□	□□	□□
Eat	■■	■■	□□	□□	□□	□□	□□	□□	□□	■■	■■	■■

Spacing:

15cm apart x 30cm between rows (6 x 12") 1cm (½") deep.

Pea

An easy to grow annual crop with several different varieties that are all cultivated in the same way. The main problem with peas is that most pests love them, hence lots of effort is used in protecting them. Depending upon variety, these plants grow to 150cm (5ft).

Care:

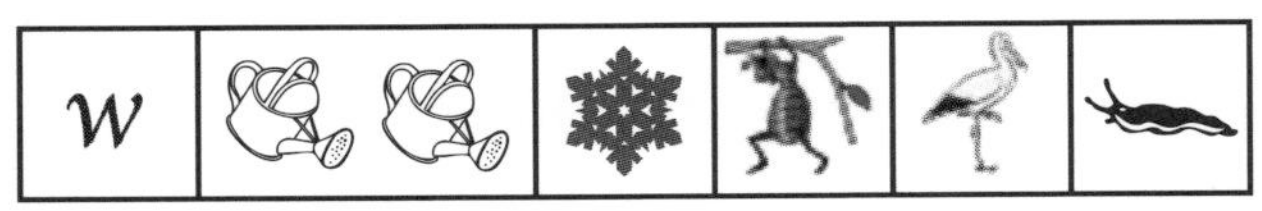

- ✔ Once seeds start to grow, insert twigs or canes in a 'V' shape each side of the row to support the scrambling plants. Tall growing types will need even more support. Netting is ideal.
- ✔ A thick mulch of grass clippings is useful to both conserve moisture round the roots and suppress any weeds.
- ✔ Pick regularly to encourage more pods.

Pests: Slugs, rabbits, mice, aphids, millipedes, weevils.

Diseases: Downy/powdery mildew, damping off, foot/root, rot, grey mould, virus diseases

Harvesting:

Pick when the pods are looking and feeling full.

Tip: Protect from birds by using twigs criss crossed over crop, netting, black thread wound around canes over the whole crop or cloches.

Site	Soil	Comments
	L 1-2	Needs humus rich soil

Approx germination	7-10 days
Planting to plate (spring sowing)	12-16 weeks
Planting to plate (autumn sowing)	30+ weeks

Sowing:

Prepare a drill, 15cm wide x 5cm (6 x 2") deep. Water and then sow one seed either side of each edge, refill the trench with soil/compost and firm down.

Planting:

	J	F	M	A	M	J	J	A	S	O	N	D
Sow												
Eat												
Sow												
Eat												
Sow												
Eat												

May/June | June/July | August | Autumn Crop

Spacing:

15cm apart x rows spaced the height of crop (6" x 24"- 5ft) approx 5cm (2") deep.

Peppers (Capsicum)

A tender half hardy annual that needs warmth and sunshine so they are generally best grown behind glass. There are now lots of peppers to choose from and depending upon variety, plants can reach approx 45-90cm (18-36").

Care:

- ✔ Keep well watered, regularly.
- ✔ Keep well supported with a cane.
- ✔ Mist daily to encourage fruit to set.
- ✔ Feed frequently (tomato food) when fruit sets.
- ✔ In very hot summers, some greenhouse shading will be beneficial.

Pests: Red spider mite, aphids, whitefly.

Diseases: Generally disease free.

Harvesting:

Pick the larger, sweet pepper type when they are green. They will ripen to orange/red within a couple of weeks. Harvest the smaller hot peppers when completely ripe.

Site	Soil	Comments
☼	Compost/Grow bags	Use good quality compost when growing in pots

Approx germination (60-70°)	12-21 days
Planting to plate	14 weeks

Sowing:

Sow the seeds in a pot of compost and keep them at a constant temperature of 60-70 °. As soon as 2 pairs of leaves have developed, prick out into individual 7cm (3") pots and grow on, still in the warmth. If you are going to keep in pots rather than using grow bags, pot on to a 13cm (5") pot when you can see the roots at the bottom and then again into a final 22cm (9") pot.

Planting:

	J		F		M		A		M		J		J		A		S		O		N		D	
Sow				pot	pot				■	■														
Eat														■	■	■	■	■						

Spacing:

Pot on into 22cm (9") pots per plant.
Alternatively plant 2-3 to a grow bag.

Potato

A tuberous perennial grown as an annual. There are 3 main types, first early, second early and main crop but within each type, there is still a lot of variety between skin colour, texture and shape. The plants take up a lot of space and will produce a crop with very little care and attention. Of course, more care and attention will reward you with a lot more produce! Depending upon variety, plants can grow between 45-90cm (18-36").

Care:

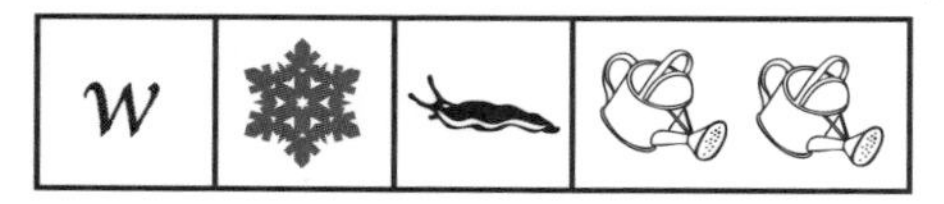

- ✔ Earth up when stem reaches 15cm (6") and again when another 15cm (6") has grown.
- ✔ Water well when tubers start to swell

Pests: Aphids, eelworms, slugs, capsid bugs, wireworms.

Diseases: Blight, scab, dry rot, internal rust, blackleg.

Harvesting:

Earlies: (June/July) Lift only as required once flowers have opened. Continues to swell well into July.

Second Earlies: (July/August) Lift as required.

Main crop: (August/September) Lift as required but before the first frosts. To store, allow stems to die down, then cut off haulm (to reduce risk of disease) and lift roots a week later. Dry off completely for 24 hours before storing in a cool dark place.

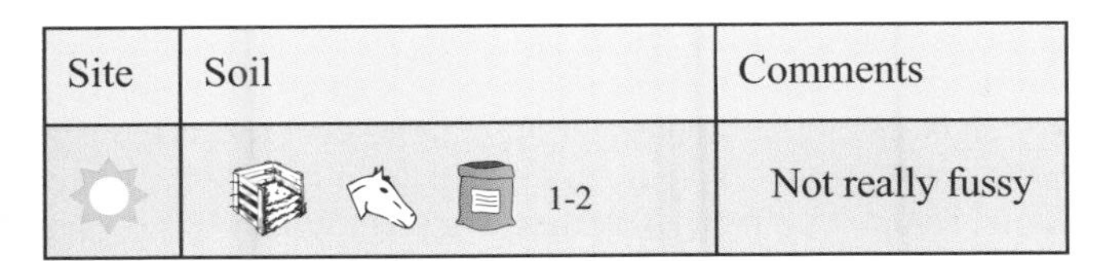

Site	Soil	Comments
	1-2	Not really fussy

Approx germination (chitting)	6 weeks
Planting to plate (earlies)	12+ weeks
Planting to plate (main crop)	22+ weeks

Sowing:

It is best to 'chit' your 'earlies' in February. Lay tubers on trays of compost in a frost free, light site until small growths appear. Tubers are ready to plant when shoots are approx 2cm (1").

Planting:

c = start chitting

	J		F		M		A		M		J		J		A		S		O		N		D	
Sow			c	c	c	■	■	■																
Eat												■	■	■	■	■	■	■						

Spacing:

Earlies:
30cm apart x 60cm between rows (1 x 2 ft), 12cm (5") deep.
Main crop:
45cm apart x 85cm between rows (1½ x 2½ft) 12cm (5") deep.

Radish

A very fast and easy to grow hardy biennial that is grown as an annual. With successional sowing, radish can be grown and harvested for many months of the year and are a particularly useful catch crop as they benefit from some shade in the heat of summer. Plants grow up to 15cm (6").

Care:

- ✔ Protect from frost.
- ✔ Water well as soon as they start to swell to encourage tender roots.

Pests: Flea beetle.

Diseases: Common scab.

Harvesting:

Summer types: Pull when needed after the radish reach an edible size. Don't leave them too long because they become woody and have a strong taste.

Winter types: Can be pulled as required when ready but will last a little longer in the soil.

Tip: The most tender roots come from fast grown radish-seeds that have had fertile soil and water.

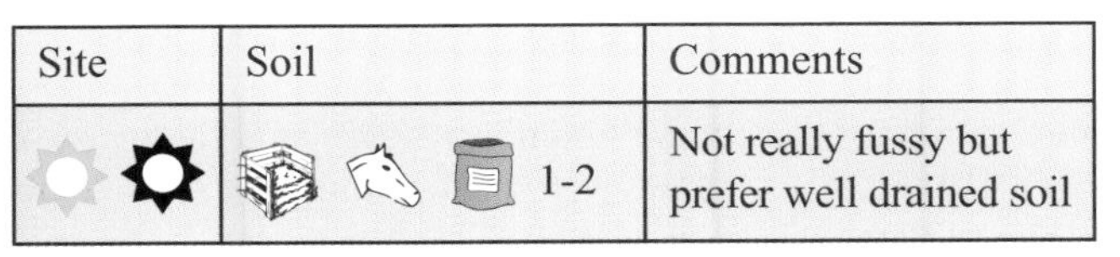

Site	Soil	Comments
	1-2	Not really fussy but prefer well drained soil

Approx germination (Chitting)	5-8 days
Planting to plate (Summer types)	4+ weeks
Planting to plate (Winter types)	10+ weeks

Sowing:

Sow very thinly in a prepared bed approx 1cm (½) deep. Thin to approx 2cm (1") for summer types and 15cm (6") winter types.

Planting:

	J	F	M	A	M	J	J	A	S	O	N	D
Sow	□□	■■	■■	■■	■■	■■	■■	□□	□□	□□	□□	□□
Eat	□□	□□	□■	■■	■■	■■	■■	■■	■■	■■	■■	□□

Spacing:

Summer types:
20cm apart x 15cm between rows (1 x 6") 1cm (½") deep.
Winter types:
15cm apart x 23cm between rows (6 x 9") 1cm (½") deep.

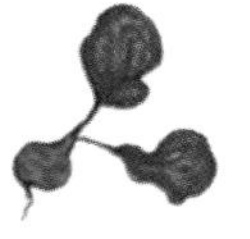

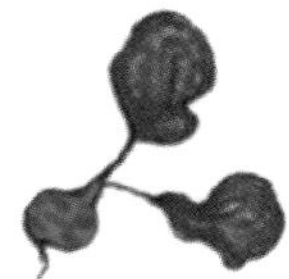

Salsify (Oyster Plant)

An unusual but easy to grow hardy perennial root crop with purple, daisy-like flowers and thin grass-like looking leaves. The pale roots are compared to a taste of peppery oysters – the older the plant the more peppery. Plants can grow up to 120cm (4ft).

Care:

- ✔ Will benefit from an application of a potash rich fertilizer.
- ✔ Do not allow to dry out; plants will be more likely to bolt and set seed.
- ✔ Weed by hand; do not disturb crowns.
- ✔ Apply a mulch to conserve moisture and reduce weeding.

Diseases: White blister.

Harvesting:

The roots should be ready from late October. Lift (with a fork) only when needed, salsify do not store very wellout of the ground. The top of a mature root should reach 5cm (2") round and you can expect roots to reach 23-30cm (9-12").

Tips: * Use fresh seed for best results.
* The young leaves can be used in salads.

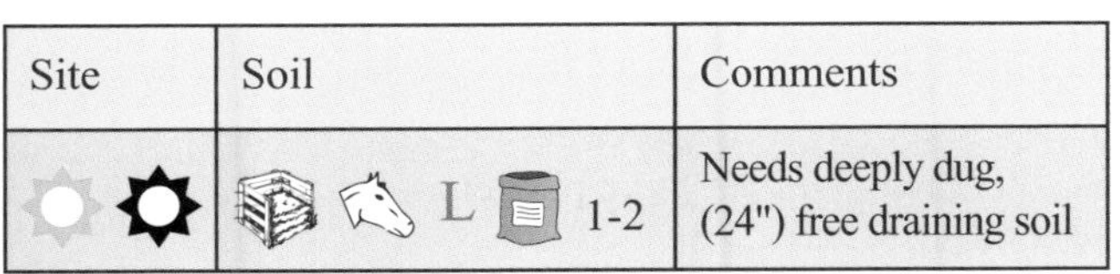

Site	Soil	Comments
	L 1-2	Needs deeply dug, (24") free draining soil

Approx germination	12-18 days
Planting to plate	20+ weeks

Sowing:

Sow very thinly in a prepared seed drill approx 1cm (½") deep. Thin to approx 15cm (6").

Planting:

	J		F		M		A		M		J		J		A		S		O		N		D	
Sow							■	■																
Eat	■	■	■	■															■	■	■	■	■	■

Spacing:

5cm apart x 30cm between rows (6 x 12") 1cm (½") deep.

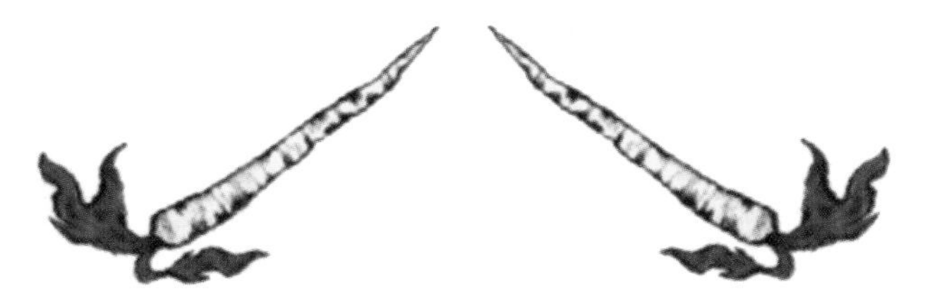

Scorzonera

An unusual but easy to grow hardy perennial root crop. It has yellow, daisy-like flowers that smell of vanilla and upright broad grass-like leaves. The dark roots have the taste of a mild parsnip. Plants can grow up to 90cm (3ft).

Care:

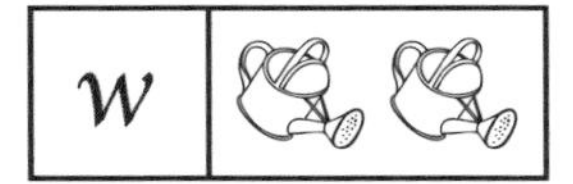

- ✔ Do not allow to dry out; plants will be more likely to bolt and set seed.
- ✔ Weed by hand, do not disturb crowns.
- ✔ Apply a mulch to conserve moisture and reduce weeding.

Diseases: White blister.

Harvesting:

The roots should be ready from late October. You can expect roots to reach 20cm (8"). Scorzonera are relatively thin and very fragile. Lift carefully, using a fork, when needed as scorzonera do not store out of the ground very well. It is thought that their taste improves with frost.

Tips: * Use fresh seed for best results.
* The young leaves can be used in salads.

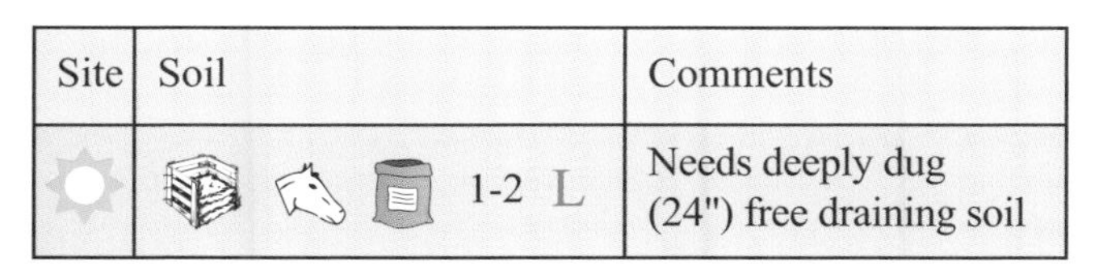

Site	Soil	Comments
	1-2 L	Needs deeply dug (24") free draining soil

Approx germination	12-18 days
Planting to plate	20+ weeks

Sowing:

Sow very thinly in a prepared seed drill approx 1cm (½") deep. Thin to approx 10cm (4").

Planting:

	J	F	M	A	M	J	J	A	S	O	N	D
Sow				■■								
Eat	■■									■■	■■	■■

Spacing:

10cm apart x 20cm between rows (4 x 8")
1cm (½") deep.

Sea Kale

A hardy perennial little known and grown, which is traditionally found around coastlines. Sea Kale with its smoky grey leaves and small white flowers will start producing from the second year after planting roots but shoots are bitter unless blanched.

Care:

- ✔ Remove all flowering stems.
- ✔ Keep well watered and liquid feed regularly.
- ✔ Sea Kale will benefit from a light salt dressing in June.
- ✔ Remove all yellowing and dying leaves.

Diseases: Club root, violet root rot.

Blanching

Once leaves have died down in November, cover the crowns with compost or leaf mould before placing a bucket over the top of the crowns. Ensure no light gets to the leaves.

Harvesting:

Leave plants to grow untouched for the first year. Once blanched in the second season, cut stalks close to the base

Plants produce well for approximately 5 years.

Tricky ****

Site	Soil	Comments
	L 1-2	Prefers humus rich, well drained sandy soil

Approx germination	14-28 days
Planting to plate	1½ years

Planting:

Plant root crowns directly into prepared bed 5cm (2") below soil surface. Sea Kale is usually forced to produce earlier crops.

	J	F	M	A	M	J	J	A	S	O	N	D
Sow				■								
Eat	■	■								■	■	■

Spacing:

60cm apart x 60cm between rows (24 x 24") 5cm (2") deep.

Spinach

Summer (annual) spinach is a hardy annual which will benefit from shade in summer. Perpetual spinach (spinach beet) is a hardy biennial. New Zealand (N/Z) types are not frost hardy and should be treated with this in mind. (See p115) Plants can grow up to 30cm (1ft).

Care:

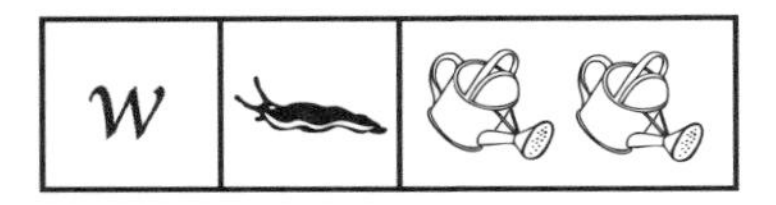

- ✔ Winter types need full sun. Summer types prefer light shade.
- ✔ Summer types need moist soil; keep well watered, they are a fast growing crop.
- ✔ Protect winter types with a cloche before first frosts.

Diseases: Cucumber mosaic virus, damping off, downy mildew, leaf spot.

Harvesting

Pick the leaves as soon as they are large enough. For summer types, the more you pick the more they grow, but you must leave central growing shoots to create more leaves. Winter types are not so fast to grow so are not quite as productive.

Tip: Grow summer spinach as a catch crop.
A perfect crop for successional sowing.

Site	Soil	Comments
	L 1-2	Needs deeply dug free draining soil

Approx germination	10-21 days
Planting to plate	12+ weeks

Sowing:

Either: Sow all types very thinly in a well watered, prepared seed drill approx 2cm (1") deep. Thin to approx 7cm (3") and again a couple of weeks later to 14cm (6"). Alternatively sow in individual cells ready for transplanting when the seedlings are approx 5cm (2") tall.

Planting:

	J	F	M	A	M	J	J	A	S	O	N	D
Sow	– / –	– / –	– / S	S / S	S / S	S / –	– / W	W / W	W / W	– / –	– / –	– / –
Eat	W / W	W / W	W / W	– / –	– / S	S / S	S / S	S / S	S / S	S / W	W / W	W / W

W = Winter; S = Summer

Spacing:

15cm apart x 30cm between rows (6 x 12") 2cm (1") deep.

Spinach (New Zealand)

New Zealand spinach (N/Z) types are half hardy annuals. They are similar to summer spinach but the leaves are smaller. Their claim to fame is that they tolerate heat better than other spinach varieties. If pinched out, plants can become quite bushy 60-90cm (24-36") and grow up to approx 30cm (1ft).

Care:

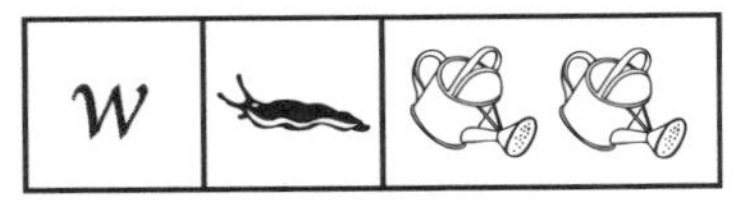

- ✔ Harden off fully before planting out.
- ✔ Pinch out growing tips regularly to promote new side shoots.
- ✔ Keep well watered.

Pests: Generally pest free.

Diseases: Generally disease free.

Harvesting

Pick lightly but regularly as soon as the leaves are large enough.

Different leaf shapes for each variety.

New Zealand

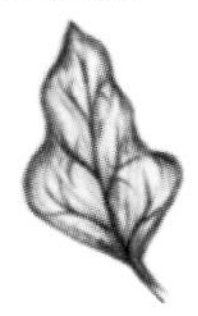

Winter

Summer

Easy *

Site	Soil	Comments
	1-2	Needs deeply dug light well drained soil

Approx germination	10-21 days
Planting to plate	12+ weeks

Sowing:

For an early start, sow in trays of compost 1cm (½") deep. Germinate and grow on under glass. Transplant into individual 7cm (3") pots and harden off before planting out. Alternatively seeds can be planted directly into prepared seed drills in May.

Planting:

	J	F	M	A	M	J	J	A	S	O	N	D
Sow												
Eat												

Spacing:

45-60cm apart x 90cm between rows (18-24 x 36") 1cm (½") deep.

Squash/Pumpkin

A half hardy annual which can trail or form a bush; there are two types, the summer and winter. These plants take up a lot of space; trailing types are particularly suitable for intercropping. Depending upon variety, plants can grow to approx 60cm (2ft) and trail until stopped.

Care:

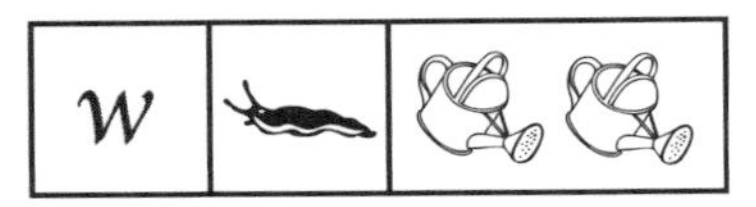

- ✔ Make sure ground is kept moist. Bury a couple of empty plant pots, which are easily filled, near the roots to make watering easier and more effective.
- ✔ Nip out the growing shoot of trailing types when 2-3 pumpkins have set.
- ✔ Once the fruits start to form, give a liquid feed at least fortnightly to maintain heavy cropping.
- ✔ Lay pumpkins on straw (etc) to keep off the ground and deter slugs/snails.

Diseases: Grey mould, mildew, mosaic virus.

Harvesting

Summer types: Cut and use when they are reach a reasonable size. Approx 12-15cm (5-6") for courgettes.

Winter types: Leave fruits to 'cure', on the vine as long as possible, harvest before first frosts. The fruits should store well for several weeks in a cool, frost free place.

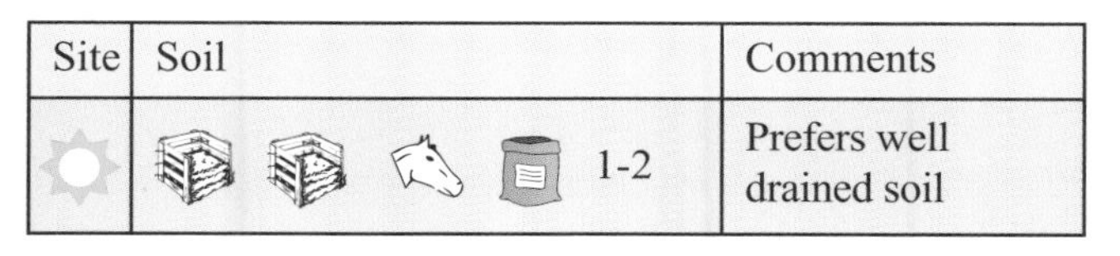

Site	Soil	Comments
	1-2	Prefers well drained soil

Approx germination	5-10 days
Planting to plate	12+ weeks

Sowing:

Either: Start off early under glass, 2 seeds, sown edgeways, to a 3" pot. Remove weaker seedling and harden off before planting out or plant 2 seeds to one outdoor station, 2cm (1") deep directly into a prepared hole.

Planting: S - Seed direct

	J		F		M		A		M		J		J		A		S		O		N		D	
Sow								pot			S													
Plant										■	■													
Eat														■	■	■	■	■	■					

Spacing:

Bush: 90cm apart x 90cm between rows (3 x 3 ft).
Trailing: 90cm apart x 150cm between rows (3 x 5ft).

Swede

A hardy biennial, grown as a useful annual winter root. Swedes belong to the brassica family and are a very easy crop to grow. Plants reach approx 30-45cm (12-18").

Care:

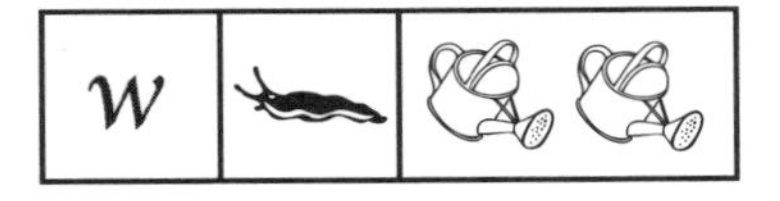

- ✔ Make sure the ground around the seedlings is reasonably firmed down.
- ✔ Keep well watered in dry periods to avoid split and woody roots.

Pests: Flea beetle, aphids, mealy aphids.
Diseases: Club root, damping off, downy mildew, soft rot.

Harvesting

Dig up when required as soon as the roots are large enough, usually any time after September. You can store Swedes in the ground over winter.

Beware: Swedes will not succeed in either an acid or recently manured soil.

Easy 

Site	Soil	Comments
	L 1-2	

Approx germination (70-80°)	7-10 days
Planting to plate	24+ weeks

Sowing:

Sow seed very thinly in a prepared seed drill directly into ground about 1cm (½") deep. Thin to approx 22cm (9") apart.

Planting:

	J		F		M		A		M		J		J		A		S		O		N		D	
Sow										■	■													
Eat	■	■	■	■	■														■	■	■	■	■	■

Spacing:

22cm apart x 37cm between rows (9 x 15") 1cm (½") deep.

Sweet Corn

Sweet corn is a half hardy maize type annual which, with careful selection of type, can be grown quite successfully in the UK. You can choose from a main crop or mini cob. Sweet corn plants can reach a very impressive 240cm (8ft)!

Care:

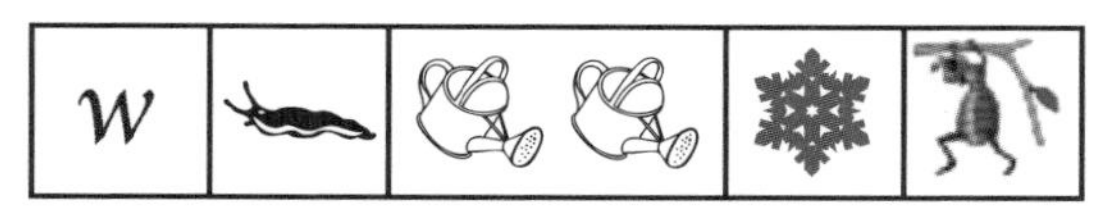

- ✔ Plant in blocks; sweet corn is wind pollinated.
- ✔ Keep earthing up any exposed basal roots which develop.
- ✔ Water generously especially as cobs are forming - to avoid only half the kernels developing/swelling.
- ✔ Give an occasional liquid feed as the cobs are developing.
- ✔ Avoid exposed sites; stake if necessary.

Pests/Diseases:

Generally trouble free.

Harvesting

Approx 4 weeks after the silks have turned brown. Test for ripeness by pulling back the outer leaves and pressing kernels, if the liquid is creamy they are ready. Expect 1-2 cobs per plant.

Beware: Mice love sweet corn seeds; they will sniff them out and devour the whole lot very quickly, even in a closed greenhouse!

Site	Soil	Comments
	1-2	Requires deeply dug, light well drained soil

Approx germination	10-15 days
Planting to plate	16 weeks

Sowing:

Preferably sow one seed per 7cm (3") pot filled with compost, under glass. Harden off before planting out. Alternatively, sow seed directly into final position, 2cm (1") deep under cloches late May.

Planting:

	J	F	M	A	M	J	J	A	S	O	N	D
Sow												
Plant												
Eat												

Spacing:

Plant in blocks, 45cm apart x 45cm between rows (18 x 18").

Be warned! Do not plant main crop and mini varieties near each other; they *will* cross pollinate – resulting in a very poor edible harvest!

Sweet Potato

An herbaceous perennial vine grown as an annual crop. It has showy convolvulus type white and purple flowers. This plant is easy to grow but needs warmth, both day and night. Plants quickly spread and if happy, vines can reach 450cm (15ft) long!

Care:

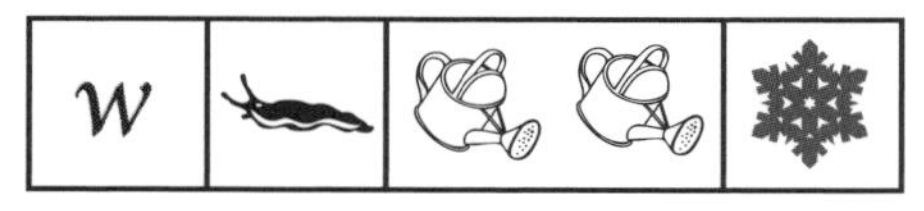

- ✔ Cover tubers in black polythene to keep soil temperatures up, weeds down and mice out.
- ✔ Do not allow to dry out; plants will split and crack.
- ✔ Leave your tubers water free for at least 3 weeks before harvesting.

Pests: Slugs, mice.

Diseases: Wireworm.

Harvesting

Dig up the roots, carefully, using a fork as soon as the leaves start to turn yellow. Tubers should be at least 10-15cm (4-6") and will mainly be found close to the surface.

Dig up and dry out in a warm place for 1-2 weeks (80ish °) before the first frosts appear.

Tip: If you cannot provide enough warmth, try growing your tubers in a very large pot in the greenhouse.

Site	Soil	Comments
	L 1-2	Prefers deeply dug free draining soil

Approx germination (chitting) (70°)	12-18 weeks
Planting to plate	20+ weeks

Sowing:

Either buy prepared 'slips' or grow your own. Use any shop bought tuber and keep approx 2cm (1") immersed in a glass of water, minimum temperature 70°. Green growths growing from the eyes of the tuber are the 'slips' which you need to cut from the tuber when they are 5-7cm (2-3") long. Pot these slips up into a 7cm (3") pot and grow on for 2-4 weeks to develop roots, still maintaining heat. Plant out at least 2 weeks after the last frost under a pre prepared ridge/tunnel of black polythene.

Planting:

c = start chitting

	J		F		M		A		M		J		J		A		S		O		N		D	
Sow				c	c		■	■	■															
Plant											■	■												
Eat																		■	■					

Spacing:

45cm apart x 90cm between rows (15 x 36") 30cm (1") deeper than soil level in pot.

Tomato (Indoor)

A tender half hardy annual that needs warmth and sunshine so they are generally best grown behind glass; even then they are a reasonably difficult crop to grow successfully. Indoor plants will climb until stopped.

Care:

- ✔ Minimum temperature 50-55°; max. temperature 80 °.
- ✔ Pinch out growing tip when it reaches top of greenhouse.
- ✔ Pinch out side shoots as soon as possible.
- ✔ Keep well tied in and supported.
- ✔ Provide lots of ventilation, open all doors, vents and windows.
- ✔ Water generously and regularly; erratic watering causes many avoidable problems.

Pests: Red spider mite, aphids, whitefly.

Diseases: Lots! (See outdoor tomatoes).

Harvesting

Pick the fruit when they are ripe.

Tips: Tomatoes will benefit from mixing a little vermiculite/ perlite in with the compost. If early enough in the season, you can root the 'pinched out' side shoots and produce fruit from your cutting.

Site	Soil	Comments
☼	Compost/Grow bags	Use good quality compost when growing in pots

Approx germination (65°)	6-10 days
Planting to plate	16 weeks

Sowing:

Sow seeds in a tray or pot of compost. Place a lid/clear bag over the top to retain moisture and keep at 65°. As soon as 1 pair of leaves has developed, prick out into individual 7cm (3") pots and grow on without the lid/bag but still in the warmth.

Planting:

Guidance given for heated ▼ and ▽ unheated greenhouses.

	J		F		M		A		M		J		J		A		S		O		N		D	
Sow		▼	▼		▽	▽	▽																	
Plant					▼	▼		▽	▽															
Eat											■	■	■	■	■	■	■	■	■					

Spacing:

Pot on into 22cm (9") pots per plant.
Alternatively plant 2-3 to a grow bag.

Tomato (Outdoor)

A half hardy annual that needs warmth and sunshine. Be sure to choose a variety that is suitable for outdoor cultivation. Not a really easy plant for outside growing if you do not have a very sunny and sheltered spot. Having said that, in many ways outdoor tomatoes are a little easier than greenhouse plants.

Care:

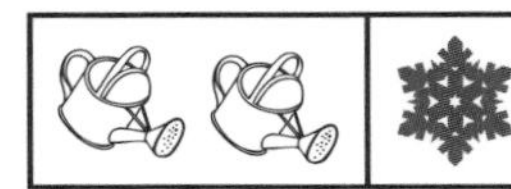

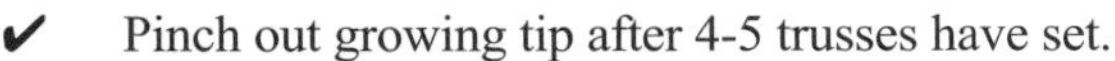

- ✔ Pinch out growing tip after 4-5 trusses have set.
- ✔ Keep well watered regularly.
- ✔ Feed frequently (tomato food) when fruit sets.
- ✔ Pick up/take off dead leaves to prevent diseases.

Pests: Red spider mite, aphids, whitefly.

Diseases: Blossom end rot, blight, viruses, leaf/ grey mould, greenback, split fruit, black rot, leaf spot, basal/stem rot.

Harvesting

Pick the fruit when ripe. Leave the small green tops attached to prolong freshness.

Tips: Bury a couple of 10cm (4") plant pots next to the plant to fill with water.

The smaller fruiting types often give better results

Site	Soil	Comments
	1-2	Prefers well drained soil ***or*** use good quality compost

Approx germination (70-80°)	7-10 days
Planting to plate	20+ weeks

Sowing:

Sow seeds in a tray or pot of compost. Place a lid/ clear bag over the top to retain moisture and keep at 65°. As soon as 2-3 pairs of leaves have developed, prick out into individual 7cm (3") pots and grow on without the lid/bag but still in the warmth.

Planting:

When your well watered plant is strong, sturdy and approx 20cm (8") plant out into either a prepared hole in the soil, approx 30cm (12") deep filled with compost, a 23cm (9") pot or 2-3 plants to a bag.

	J		F		M		A		M		J		J		A		S		O		N		D	
Sow						■	■																	
Plant											■													
Eat															■	■	■	■						

Spacing:

45 cm apart x 60cm between rows (18 x 24") 2cm (1") deep.

Turnip

A half-hardy biennial, grown as an annual root. Turnips belong to the brassica family and are a very easy crop to grow. There are three main types; the round, flat and long rooted. All roots taste mildly mustardy. Plants reach approx 30-45cm (12-18")

Care:

- ✔ Make sure the ground around the seedlings is kept reasonably firm.
- ✔ Keep well watered in dry periods to avoid split and woody roots.

Pests: Flea beetle, aphids.

Diseases: Club root, damping off, downy mildew, violet root rot.

Harvesting

Pull and use summer turnips when young and immature. Main crop or winter turnips can be harvested when needed from October onwards, they will store well in the ground.

Tip: Cut green leaves from main crop turnips in March and use the new growth as fresh greens.

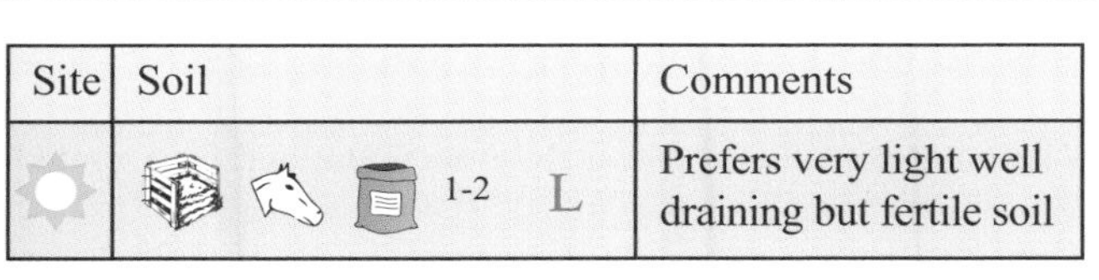

Site	Soil	Comments
	1-2 L	Prefers very light well draining but fertile soil

Approx germination (70-80°)	7-10 days
Planting to plate (Summer types)	8+ weeks
Planting to plate (Winter types)	14+ weeks

Sowing:

Sow seed very thinly in a pre watered, prepared seed drill directly into ground about 1cm (½") deep. Thin to approx 22cm (8") apart.

Planting:

	J	F	M	A	M	J	J	A	S	O	N	D
Sow	□□	□□	□■	■■	■■	□□	□□	□□	□□	□□	□□	□□
Eat	■■	■□	□□	□□	□□	□□	□□	□□	□□	■■	■■	■■

Spacing:

Early: 11cm apart x 23cm between rows (4 x 9").
Main crop: 20cm apart x 30cm between rows (8 x 12").

Pest and Disease Controls

There are many things that can be easily incorporated into your general routine to help prevent pests and diseases without resorting to strong chemicals that often do not discriminate between friends and foes.

You will find that, if allowed and encouraged, your plot will build up a whole range of beneficial insects and predators very quickly.

1. Prepare ground thoroughly

By regular digging and generally taking good care of your soil, you may notice particular pests and can take action. Some pests do not like to be in ground that is regularly 'poked' and will often move on. Lastly, by digging over your soil, birds will take advantage of any free food in the form of pests that you present.

In addition, if you have heavy, slow draining soils, the addition of compost and regular digging will reduce the risk of rot due to the roots/crops standing in cold and waterlogged soil.

2. Practice crop rotation

Disease will have a harder time taking hold; Nutrients will be evenly used reducing the problem of build up.

3. Avoid overcrowding

Plants need good air circulation to help repel disease.

4. Choose seeds carefully

Opt for disease resistant varieties if you know you have a particular problem.

5. Use barriers

Netting, mesh, cloches, fleece and collars will all help to prevent pest infestations. Select the most appropriate for the job.

Netting will keep birds off, meshes will keep smaller insects as well as birds away. Cloches will help prevent flying insects and slugs moving in. Cardboard or old carpet collars (cut in circles) placed around plant stems will help to repel/confuse soil borne pests and root flies, many of which prefer to lay their eggs around the roots underground. You can also try recycling your old plastic bottles. Simply cut the top and bottom off and use as a cuff; bear in mind the final width of the stalk.

6. General tidiness

Be fastidious in clearing away fallen plant debris. Pests hide in fallen plant debris and diseases easily start in decaying matter.

7. Keep areas well weeded

Weeds need moisture and nutrients to survive. If they take them from your crops, your plants will have to fight harder for what they need and will be weakened.

Also, overgrown areas harbour pests and diseases, you are providing them with their own little safe haven.

8. Scare tactics

Old CD's hung on string over rows of crops and plastic bottles on sticks placed amongst rows will provide some protection.

9. Use traps

Pheromone, grease, sticky and beer traps can all play a part in catching pests before they become a serious problem.

10. Companion planting

See more in the companion planting section.

11. Encourage friends

Try to provide habitats for useful predators. A few stones will provide a hiding place for newts, toads and ground beetles. Artificial nesting boxes, strategically placed around your plot, can also be a useful addition for insects like lacewings and hoverflies.

12. Be vigilant

Quite often if you can spot a pest early action can be taken. In the simplest terms, if you see a caterpillar, pick it off.

13. Provide water

Rather a luxury for many, but a small, shallow pond will attract an abundance of wildlife. It doesn't have to be big to be effective.

Aphids

There are many types (green, black, mealy etc) but they are all guilty of increasing rapidly and sucking the sap from plants, creating a sticky secretion, which then encourages sooty moulds. Aphids also transmit virus disease.

Rub aphids off (the ones you can get!) with your fingers, and water plant with a solution of washing up liquid.

Asparagus Beetles

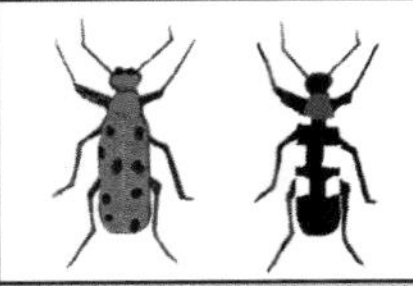

From June onwards, adult beetles and their larvae eat asparagus foliage overnight. They overwinter in the soil to do the same again next year.

Capsid Bugs

These bugs come in different shapes, sizes and colours. Both adults and nymphs suck the sap from new and tender growth. They also inject poisonous saliva that kills the affected plant tissue. Leaves are left distorted and shredded. Some types overwinter in garden debris.

Pick off any bugs you can spot, and water with a solution of diluted washing up liquid.

Caterpillars

Are an absolute menace! Caterpillars devour leaves very quickly, leaving just spines. Eggs are easy to spot and are normally found on the undersides of leaves. (The eggs of the Cabbage White are yellow and are laid in clusters). By growing a few nettles nearby you can sometimes provide an alternative breeding ground.

Rub eggs off. Pick off caterpillars. Netting helps to stop butterflies getting on the plant to begin with.

Cabbage Root Fly

It is difficult to distinguish between some of the flies; you generally have to guess, working with the crop that has been attacked and the resulting damage. Mature cabbage root flies are most active in April/May. They lay eggs in the soil, which develop into 7mm (¼") creamy coloured grubs which then tunnel into the roots of all brassicas and remain in the soil until next year. Soil collars may help.

Carrot Root Fly

7mm (¼") creamy coloured grubs bore tunnels and feed on the roots of carrots, parsnips, celeriac, parsley etc. The mature flies are most active in June where they lay their eggs in the soil. The adult carrot fly is a low flyer so it is often possible to avoid attacks if plants are grown in beds 60cm high.

Companion planting is useful for this pest. Alternatively use fine mesh or fleece to avert problems.

Celery Fly

This tiny fly is responsible for very small, white, leaf mining grubs that tunnel between the leaf tissues of celery and parsnip-like plants leaving a sort of transparent trail within the leaf itself that then turn brown.

Pick off any leaves showing the tell tale signs and burn.

Chafer Grub and Beetles

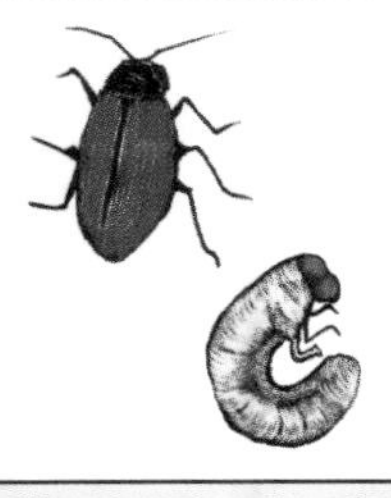

Grubs are fat and a creamy white colour with a coloured head approx 2cm (1"). They live in the soil for 2 seasons before reaching maturity and usually present themselves in a 'C' shape. Feeding on roots throughout the year, they cause extensive damage. The adults themselves feed mainly on leaves and can also cause extensive damage.

Encourage natural predators, turn over soil at every opportunity to expose to the birds or hunt for them yourself in soil around the affected roots!

Cutworms

Cutworms are immature moths (caterpillars) that live in the soil. They will happily eat leaves and foliage but tend to stay lower down and sever stems. Feeding mainly at night, they are fat, and greeny brown in colour.

Help to prevent their appearance by putting little collars around the stem of the plants likely to be affected and providing less breeding areas by keeping weeds down. Alternatively, you can search for the grub in the top 2-3cm (1-1½") of soil around affected plants.

Earwigs (also see friends)

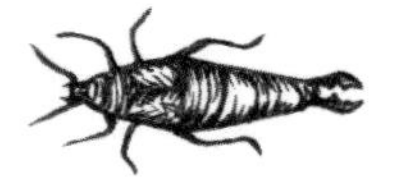

Love dahlias, beetroot and parsnip leaves. They feed at night and can devour the leaf or at best leave it full of ragged holes.

If earwigs are a problem, fill a 3" pot with straw and place upside down on a stick near the problem area. Earwigs will be found hiding in the straw – you should check and remove daily.

Eelworms

Eelworms are microscopic (and transparent) measuring in at 1/25". They live within the plant tissue and increase rapidly causing discolouration and deformities of the leaves.

Completely remove any affected plant (including the soil around it) and burn.

New Zealand Flat Worms

Live on earthworms. This flat 'worm' is covered in a sticky slime and has a purple-brown body with caramel coloured underside. When extended it can reach 12cm (5"). Prefers damp hiding spots.

Adult ground beetles are a natural predator that can be encouraged. Adding organic matter to soil will increase earth worm populations.

Flea Beetles

There are lots of different varieties but each type eats holes in leaves of leafy vegetables, turnips and swede. They seem to be most active on bright sunny days and overwinter in plant debris.

Make sure you clear away all debris from your plot to reduce the overwintering areas.

Leatherjackets

The larvae of crane fly, (daddy long legs). They are fat, dark grey-brown grubs, approx 2cm (1") long. They live in the soil and feed on roots. More of a problem on newly cultivated plots where there has been a build up of grassland.

Larger birds love leatherjackets. Dig over the soil in affected areas and the birds will help reduce numbers.

Leaf Miner

See celery fly.

Mealy Aphids

This serious pest has an appearance all of its own. Large colonies of tiny, grey, waxy 'bugs' increase rapidly, forming a powdery grey clump. As all aphids, they suck the sap from plants creating a sticky secretion, which then encourages sooty moulds and virus infections. These pests thrive in warm greenhouses but they can also frequently be found on the undersides of leaves.

Rub off immediately upon detection. Thoroughly water and spray affected plant with a solution of dilute washing up liquid. If the attack has gone unnoticed and has become very severe it really is best to just destroy the whole plant to avoid even more spreading.

Millipede

Millipedes like damp and moist conditions. They feed on debris and dead plant matter but will move on to roots and tunnel into tubers. They are not to be confused with the 'good' centipede – they have twice the amount of legs and are not as fast.

Make sure you keep your plot free of debris and suitable conditions for this pest to thrive – millipedes can live for up to 7 years.

Onion Fly

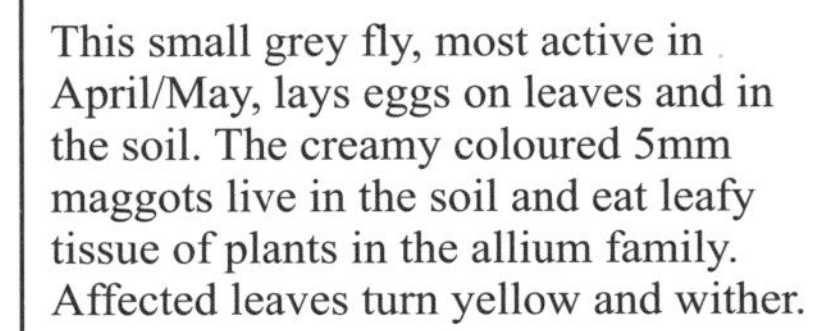

This small grey fly, most active in April/May, lays eggs on leaves and in the soil. The creamy coloured 5mm maggots live in the soil and eat leafy tissue of plants in the allium family. Affected leaves turn yellow and wither.

Completely lift and remove affected plants and some surrounding soil to help prevent the maggots spreading further.

Red Spider Mite

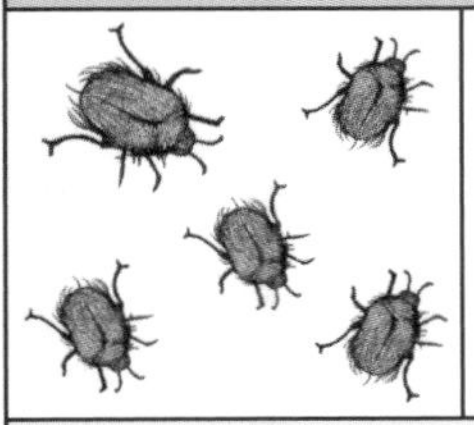

This miniscule pest, which leaves fine webbed strands over leaves, is mainly a problem for greenhouses and containers. Mites very rapidly set up colonies that suck sap from leaves encouraging viruses and sooty moulds.

Spider mites do not like moist conditions; they need arid air to reproduce. Discourage a mild attack by spraying affected areas with cold water 2-3 times daily. Spider mites will quickly invade neighbouring plants so sticky traps are also a good idea.

Pea Moth (Maggot)

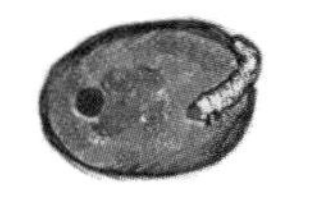

Pea maggots tunnel through pods and into peas leaving then inedible.

Pick off and burn affected pods.

Slugs/Snails

Eat everything! Mainly at night leaving tell tale holes, or remnants of seedlings and slimy trails. Different varieties live both above and below the soil.

There are many ways to reduce the slug and snail population – everyone has their favourite method! My preferences, after keeping things really debris free around the plot and encouraging frogs, toads and newts, is to trail a wide band of sand and dry oats around seedlings at risk. These devastating and nuisance pests do not like to crawl over the scratchy sand and if they do, they then eat the oats, which swell. You do have to keep replacing the oats - especially after rain when they become relatively ineffective (just when you need them most). Other suggestions include little dishes of beer, (replaced regularly) shallow moats around seed beds, cut off plastic bottles, petroleum jelly, broken egg shells, salt trails, to list a few.

Thrips (Thunder Fly)

Are very small black insects which feed by piercing the leaf tissue and sucking the sap from the leaf. Thrips are most troublesome with peas. The tell tale sign (apart from an instant cloud of black flies when the leaves are disturbed) is a silvery speckling on leaves.

If a solution of dilute washing up liquid doesn't work very effectively you may have to resort to an organic remedy.

Weevils (Pea and Bean Weevil shown)

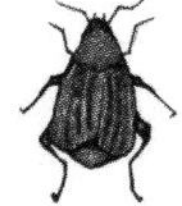

Weevils are very difficult to control. You can try to hunt them yourself – birds really love them but it is likely that you will have to resort to an organic remedy.

Whiteflies

There are normally so many of these little flies they seem to appear in clouds! They live on the undersides of leaves and suck the sap from leaves secreting a sticky substance like aphids.

Water and spray affected plant with a solution of washing up liquid.

Wireworms

Wireworms are young click beetles. They are long and are shiny orangey coloured. They mainly live in recently cultivated soil feeding on roots and tunnelling into tubers and stems.

Woodlice

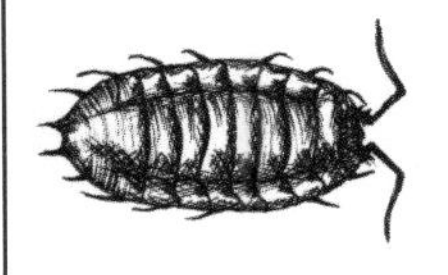

These grey, hard-shelled 1cm (½") long pests hide away in dark places. They feed at night and cause damage to roots, stems and leaves.

If Woodlice are a problem, fill a 3" pot with straw and place on its side near the problem area. Woodlice will be found hiding in the straw – you should check and remove daily

Bigger Pests

Mice	
	Mice especially love peas and some larger seeds.
	You can cover newly sown rows of seeds outside with cloches until they emerge. In the greenhouse, you can cover pots and trays with a plastic bag or lid. Maybe consider growing a few extra plants to make up for the peas you will loose.
Birds	
	Pigeons: Strip all the green from the leaves just leaving the leaf skeleton Blackbirds: eat your ripe fruit. Small birds: eat/dig up seeds and seedlings.
	Tie black cotton to sticks all around the rows, approx 2 and 5cm high, for lowecrops and use netting, for larger plants, to stop birds attacking your crops.
Rabbits	
	Devour rows of plants very quickly leaving you with nothing at all on smaller plants and just a clean cut stem or stalk on larger plants.
	Use wire netting, at least 90cm (3ft) high and buried at least 30cm (12") below the soil.
Moles	
	Possibly attracted by a plentiful supply of worms in a well-tended plot, moles cause havoc when tunnelling. Consider purchasing a sonic mole deterrent.

Ladybirds (+ larvae)	
	Devour aphids, mealy bugs and small insects.
	Encourage these insects by providing habitats where they can survive.
Hoverflies	
	No larger than 1cm (½"), hoverflies, unlike wasps, do not sting or bite. They prefer to devour aphids, mealy bugs and small insects.
	Encourage these insects by growing flowers on your plot and providing habitats where they can survive.
Lacewings	
	Devour aphids, mealy bugs and small insects.
	Encourage these insects by providing habitats where they can survive.
Ground Beetles	
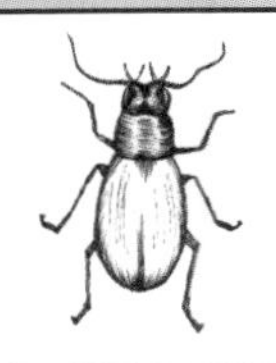	These big shiny black beetles love to feast on slugs, root aphid types and some underground pests.
	Encourage these visitors by providing hiding places such as stones.

Parasitic Wasps

Prey on caterpillars, aphids and even the odd cockroach.

Encourage these non stinging, soft bodied, useful friends by providing a sheltered site. Plants that will attract are cosmos, parsley, carrots, hairy vetch and plants from the sunflower family.

Centipedes

Happily eat slugs, snails, spiders, mites, beetles and woodlice.

Centipedes are difficult to attract, but you can encourage the ones that may be resident on your plot to stay by providing a plank of wood. Centipedes are one of the few friends that can be provoked into biting humans.

Earwig

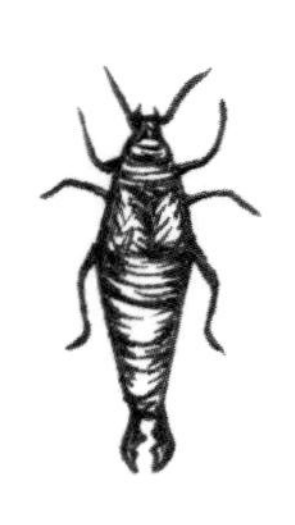

Eat caterpillars, aphids and some types of insect eggs at night. Throughout the day they hide. The males have the more curved pincers.

If you really want to attract earwigs, just leave a few stones or a pile of rotting wood on your plot, the female earwig will lay approx 80 eggs in a nest!

Frogs/Toads/Newts	
	Love slugs and snails. An adult toad can eat about 10,000 insects in one year!
	Toads, frogs and newts all need water to survive. If you can, provide a shallow pond area to encourage these creatures. (Provide some sort of ramp as an escape route for less able visitors.) A cool hiding place for the day will also be appreciated, a pile of stones, logs or even a plank of wood (for toads) are all acceptable.
Hedgehogs	
	Are nocturnal and love slugs and snails.
	Hedgehogs are in decline. If you are lucky enough to have hedgehogs around, keep a small area with a pile of leaves, logs to encourage them to stay. Avoid any use of slug pellets which will poison the hedgehogs themselves – let the hedgehogs eat your slugs for you!
Worms	
	Are an essential link to a healthy balanced plot. They tunnel through the soil which helps to aerate and water; their castings also enrich the existing soil. Earthworms are also an important part of many friendly predators' diets. Encourage them by adding plenty of organic matter - you will be well rewarded for your efforts.

Botrytis/Grey Mould	
	A fungal disease whose spores are airborne. The infection gets in through wounds on the plant and is a bigger problem in damp summers. It resembles a fluffy mould which when disturbed releases clouds of spores, which then infect everything around it.
	Aim for good air circulation and remove any debris around plants. Remove and burn anything which has botrytis.
Cankers	
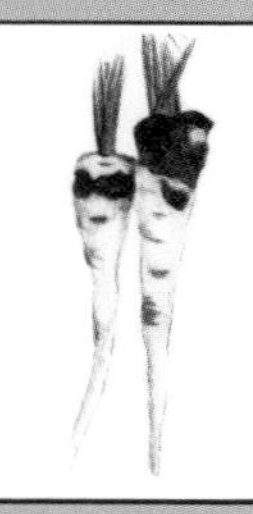	Both a fungal and bacterial problem that affects parsnips causing the roots to rot away. Canker will also show itself on leaves later in the season.
	There is no cure, affected roots need to be destroyed. Prevention: practise crop rotation. Make sure plants are not overcrowded and lime the soil if needed.
Chocolate Spot	
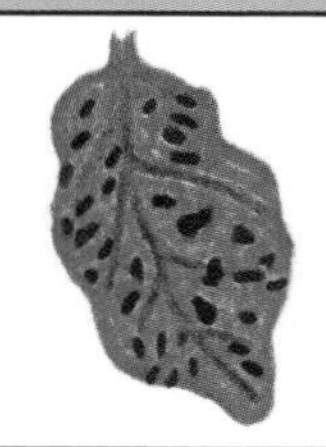	Is a fungal disease, which mainly affects broad beans in humid weather. Spots usually start to appear in June and July, but chocolate spot may also affect overwintering plants in December/January.
	Destroy affected leaves. Prevention: good drainage and avoid overcrowding.

Club Root	
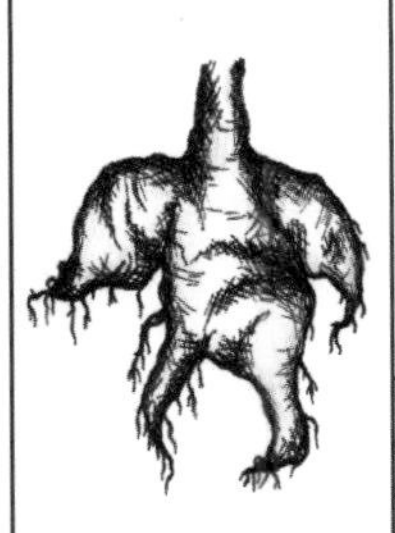	A serious fungal disease mainly attacking brassicas. More common on acid soils, club root distorts roots making them appear very swollen. Leaves will become discoloured and wilt in hot weather. Once present, club root can last for 10 years or more.
	There is no treatment for club root. Lift diseased plants and burn. Do not grow brassicas in the same space for several years. Make sure there is both enough drainage and lime content in the soil.

(Cucumber) Mosiac Virus	
	Is a virus disease, which affects many different vegetables. Microscopic particles enter through a wound in a plant causing distortion, discoloration, mottling, wilting and little growth. Greenfly are the main source of infection.
	There is no treatment. Lift diseased plants and burn. Viruses will spread rapidly. Try to keep on top of aphids.

Downy Milldew	
	Downy mildew is a fungal disease, which thrives in cool, moist conditions. The top of the leaf has yellowish patches and underneath the leaf is a grey-white fluffy growth. Quite quickly, the patches will turn brown and drop.
	Pick off and destroy infected leaves. Prevention: avoid overcrowding and bad drainage. Remove any old plant debris, which may harbour spores to re-infect other plants.
Eelworm	
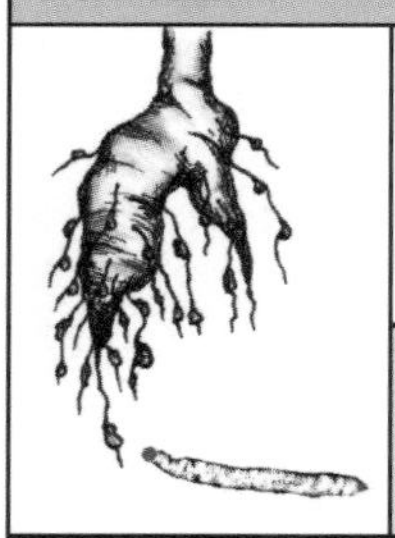	Eelworms are microscopic (and transparent) measuring in at 1/25". They live within the plant tissue and increase rapidly causing discolouration and deformities of the leaves and roots.
	Completely remove any affected plant (including the soil around it) and burn
Gummosis	
	Gummosis is a disease mainly found in cucumbers. The brown spots eating into the fruit secrete a sticky substance. This ailment is generally caused by wet and cold conditions and poor air circulation.
	Pick off and destroy any affected fruits. Prevention: Increase both warmth and air circulation.

<table>
<tr><td colspan="2">Halo Blight</td></tr>
<tr><td rowspan="2">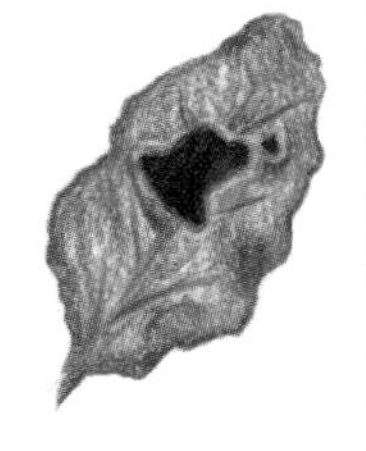</td><td>A bacterial disease brought in on seeds. Mainly found on podded vegetables, in cold wet seasons. A yellow ring develops around a brown spot and growth is stunted.</td></tr>
<tr><td>Lift and destroy affected plants. Do not grow the same crop on affected site for at least 2 years.</td></tr>
<tr><td colspan="2">Leaf Spot</td></tr>
<tr><td rowspan="2">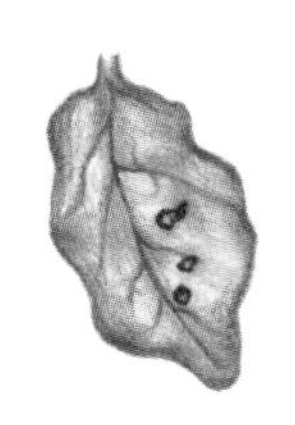</td><td>Both a fungal and bacterial infection, leaf spot generally stays with one particular type of plant when it arrives – generally peas or beans. Cool wet conditions encourage this disease. It can also affect the pods.</td></tr>
<tr><td>Pick off and burn affected leaves. Do not grow the same crop on affected site for at least 2 years.</td></tr>
<tr><td colspan="2">Leaf Mould</td></tr>
<tr><td rowspan="2">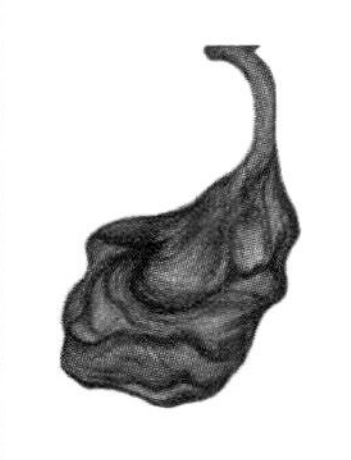</td><td>Leaf mould is just a general description of any fungal growth on rotting plant matter. Mould appears when conditions are cold and damp and air circulation is poor.</td></tr>
<tr><td>Avoid overcrowding, improve air circulation and raise temperatures if plants in a greenhouse are affected.</td></tr>
<tr><td>Lettuce Virus</td><td>See Cucumber Mosaic Virus.</td></tr>
</table>

Milldew	See Powdery Mildew.
Potato Blight	
	A fungal disease, which shows itself as brown marks on leaves and stem in both potatoes and tomatoes. It is most common in June and July. In wet weather fungal spores can actually be seen on the underside of affected leaves.
	Pick off and burn affected leaves. Prevention: check you are planting healthy tubers. This disease will overwinter. Avoid overcrowding and water at ground level.
Potato Scab	
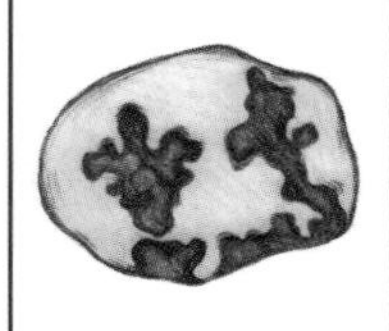	A range of fungal diseases that are more prevalent in wet weather and on badly draining soil. (Although common scab is usually worse under dry conditions on light soils). All is not lost with scab, you can still eat the potato – after peeling off skin.
	Prevention: pay attention to the soil condition; add plenty of organic matter.
Powdery Mildew	
	There are various types of powdery mildew, some attack a particular crop but there are others that are not so fussy. All produce a white powdery coat of spores on both leaves and stems, which appears May to September.
	Lift and destroy affected plants. Prevention: improve air circulation and keep plants well watered.

Rust	
	A common fungus which attacks a range of plants, particularly leeks. Rust initially presents yellow spots on leaves which rapidly changes to bright orange patches. If left, these spores will spread to nearby susceptible plants.
	Prevention: pay attention to the soil condition; add plenty of organic matter. Remove all affected leaves. If a bad attack, remove and burn the whole plant to stop the spread. Prevention: avoid the site for susceptible crops for at least 1 season.
Soft Rot	
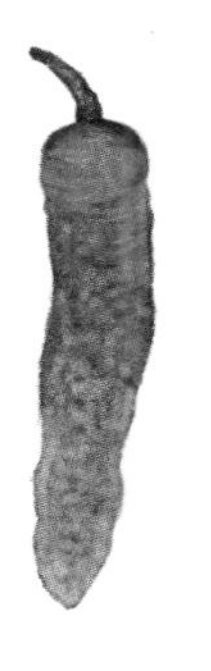	Soft rot is both a bacterial and fungal disease. It causes serious decay and enters through damaged tissues resulting in just a slimy mush. In the ground it is most common in poor draining soils. During storage moist/damp conditions will usually result in soft rot.
	Destroy all affected produce. Prevention: improve drainage in soils; store only healthy produce in airy conditions.

Stem/Basal Rot	
	A fungal disease which results in a brown sunken area on the base of the stem and turns lower leaves yellow. The most common cause are the spores of grey mould.
	Lift and burn all affected stems as soon as possible to stop the spread. Prevention: see botrytis.

Violet Root Rot	
	A fungus that is soil borne that mostly appears in badly draining acid soils. It produces violet fungal threads which will eventually cover roots, crowns and stems of an infected plant - especially asparagus. The spores from the threads will last in the affected area for many years.
	Lift up (with surrounding soil) and burn any infected plants/tubers. It is best to plant green manures on the site or leave fallow. Do not plant any crop susceptible to violet root rot for at least 5 years.

White Blister	
	Is a fungal disease which has glistening white patches on leaves, which if left, will cover the whole plant.
	Cut off and burn affected leaves. Prevention: avoid overcrowding and practise crop rotation.

It's not a pest or a disease - what else could it be?

Pests and diseases are, to some degree, out of our control. There are however many frustrating ailments which when armed with a little knowledge are possible to reduce.

Black Rot
A problem mainly found in stored root vegetables.
Black shrunken marks appear over the root.
Store vegetables in a well ventilated place.

Blown Sprouts
Sprouts which have loose and opened leaves instead of a tight cluster.
Possible causes are the plant roots not being secure enough in the ground, or not enough organic matter in the soil.
Make sure there is plenty of organic matter available and that soil around the roots is well packed down.

Bolting
Bolting is where a plant 'runs to seed' before it should.
There are several possibilities: seeds sown too early or late, a shortage of water, overcrowding or shortage of organic matter.

Frost
Leaves and shoots will turn black but probably recover; younger plants will be killed completely, and if frost reaches the roots of mature plants, the whole plant may well die.

Ensure that the roots on overwintering plants are well covered with soil. Make sure your frost tender plants are not put out too early. Protect young plants and leaves with fleece if a frost is expected.

Fanging
A problem where roots 'fork'.
Often caused by growing in either freshly manured ground where the soil is too rich and the plant tries to do too much or the ground has stones.
See crop rotation charts and make sure ground is free from debris.

Green Tops
Caused by sunlight reaching the roots of carrots/potatoes etc.
Make sure that crops are well covered at all times.

Shade (Too much)
Shade produces scraggy, leggy plants that are weak and will not perform well.

Sun Scald/Tipburn
Light brown tissue-like patches around the edges of leaves.
Contact with very bright light/hot sun, worse in greenhouses where temperatures are magnified.
Provide some shading if possible; raise humidity levels in the greenhouse.

Thick Neck
This problem mainly affects onions. The neck of the plant becomes very thick and the bulbs below stop growing. Often associated with over rich ground, especially too much Nitrogen.

Wind
There are two main problems with wind: wind rock and cold winds.
Wind Rock will dislodge roots causing them to be exposed to a whole host of pests and diseases. Very cold winds in the early spring/summer mainly cause leaf damage but can also kill young seedlings if not hardened off properly.

Wire Stem
Stems become black and shrivelled.
Generally caused by roots standing in wet and cold soil or compost.
Do not overwater or be tempted to plant out early.

Whiptail
Leaves are unusually thin and straggly.
This problem is generally caused by acidic soil conditions. Make sure the plot is properly limed before sowing or planting.

Splitting
Roots, cabbage heads, celery hearts etc split.
Mainly caused by over watering after a dry spell.
Do not allow crops in the ground to dry out. Water regularly and evenly.

Quick month by month sowing and planting checklist

This guide is general. It is very important to be aware of your regional weather variations as soil and weather conditions differ considerably throughout the country – eg frost lingers longer in the North. Seeds sown into cold wet soil will rot and you will need to start again.

▼ Sow under glass ▽ Heated greenhouse

⌂ Outdoors under a cloche

FEBRUARY

Sow		Plant
Broad Beans	▽	Jerusalem Artichokes
Kohl Rabi ⌂	Lettuce	Garlic
Peas ⌂	Radish	Globe Artichokes
	▼	Onion sets
	Onions	Shallots

MARCH

Sow		Plant
Beetroot ⌂		Asparagus
Broad Beans	Celery ▼	Jerusalem Artichokes
Leeks	Onions	Onions/Shallots
Carrots ⌂		Potatoes
Cauliflower		Garlic
Kohl Rabi ⌂		

Parsnips		
Peas	Aubergine	
Radish	Cucumber	
Spinach	Peppers	
Sprouts	Tomatoes	
Turnips		

APRIL

Sow		**Plant**
Beetroot	Celery	Asparagus
Broad Beans	Onions	Potatoes
Broccoli		
Cabbage		
Carrots		
Cauliflower	Aubergine	
Chard	Celery	
French Beans	Outdoor Cucumber	
Kale		
Kohl Rabi		
Leeks		
Lettuce		
Parsnips		
Peas		
Radish		
Spinach		
Sprouts		

MAY

Sow		Plant
Beetroot	Celery	Celeriac
Broad Beans	Courgette	Celery
Broccoli		Leeks
Calabrese	Beans	Peppers
Cabbage	Marrows	Sprouts
Cauliflower	Onions	Tomatoes
Chard	Pumpkins	
Chicory	Squash	
Kale	Sweetcorn	
French Beans		
Kale		
Kohl Rabi	Aubergine	
Leeks	Cucumber	
Peas		
Radish		
Spinach		
Sprouts		
Turnips		
Salads		
Swedes		

JUNE

Sow	Plant
Beetroot	Beans
Brocoli/ Calabrese	Brassicas
Cabbage	Celeriac
Carrots	Celery
Cauliflower	Leeks
Chard	Sprouts
Endive	
Kale	Aubergine
French Beans	Cucumber
Kale	Peppers
Kohl Rabi	Tomatoes
Leeks	
Peas	
Radish	
Runner Beans	
Spinach	
Sprouts	
Turnips	
Salads	
Swedes	
Sweetcorn	

JULY

Sow	Plant
Beetroot	All Brassicas
Cabbage (Spring)	Cabbage (Savoy)
Carrots	Cauliflower
Chicory	Celeriac
Chinese Cabbage	Celery
French Beans	Kale
Kale	Leeks
Kohl Rabi	Orientials
Peas	Sprouts
Radish	
Spinach	
Salads	
Spinach	
Turnips	

AUGUST

Sow	Plant
Cabbage (Spring)	Cabbage (Savoy)
Carrots	Kale
Chicory	Orientals
Chinese cabbage	
French Beans	
Kale	
Kohl Rabi	
Radish	
Spinach	
Spring onions	
Salads	
Spinach	
Turnips	

SEPTEMBER

Sow	Plant
Chard	Cabbage
Spinach	Chicory
Salads	Kale
Spinach	Orientals
Winter Lettuce	Radicchio
Corn Salad	Spinach

October

Sow	Plant
Broad Beans	Garlic
Peas	Onion sets
Quick Growing ⌂ Salads	
Corn Salad ⌂	

November

Sow	Plant
Broad Beans	Garlic
Peas	Onion sets

Vitamin and Mineral Chart

Now you have grown all these lovely veggies, what vitamins and minerals do they have in them? (Information given for the most popular).

Highest amount contained

Middling amount contained

Small/trace amounts contained

per one cupful / **per half*	Vitamin A	Vitamin B1	Vitamin B2	Vitamin B6	Vitamin C	Vitamin E	Vitamin K	Folate	Niacin	Calcium	Iron	Manganese	Magnesium	Phosphorus	Potassium	Sodium	Selenium	Copper	Zinc
Artichoke																			
Asparagus*																			
Aubergine																			
Runner Beans																			
Beetroot																			
Broccoli*																			
B. Sprouts																			
Cabbages*																			
Carrot*																			
Cauliflower*																			
Celeriac																			
Celery																			
Chard																			
Chicory																			

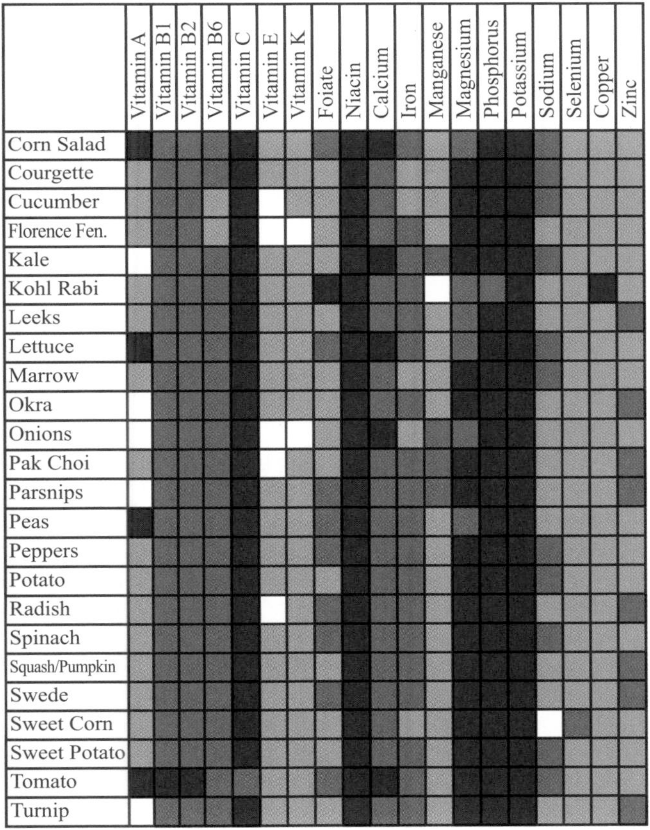

	Vitamin A	Vitamin B1	Vitamin B2	Vitamin B6	Vitamin C	Vitamin E	Vitamin K	Foiate	Niacin	Calcium	Iron	Manganese	Magnesium	Phosphorus	Potassium	Sodium	Selenium	Copper	Zinc
Corn Salad																			
Courgette																			
Cucumber																			
Florence Fen.																			
Kale																			
Kohl Rabi																			
Leeks																			
Lettuce																			
Marrow																			
Okra																			
Onions																			
Pak Choi																			
Parsnips																			
Peas																			
Peppers																			
Potato																			
Radish																			
Spinach																			
Squash/Pumpkin																			
Swede																			
Sweet Corn																			
Sweet Potato																			
Tomato																			
Turnip																			

Index

Notes